Puffin Books
Editor: Kaye Webb

THE YOUNG PUFFIN BOOK OF CROSSWORDS

Crosswords are great fun to do, but at first the concept can be confusing and hard to grasp. In this book Mavis Cavendish starts right at the beginning explaining how to put the letters into boxes to form words, and how words are fitted together to form crosswords. All the word objects have been carefully chosen to be instantly recognized by young children and as the child gets more proficient, the crosswords get more complex, moving away from the basic picture–word link to simple clues, the more complicated standard crossword clues and the different sorts of words found in crosswords.

The Young Puffin Book of Crosswords is a lively and absorbing introduction to words and crosswords, for children of 5 (with the help of their parents or teachers) to 10 (on their own).

Mavis Cavendish

Illustrated by Stuart Kettle

The Young Puffin Book of **Crosswords**

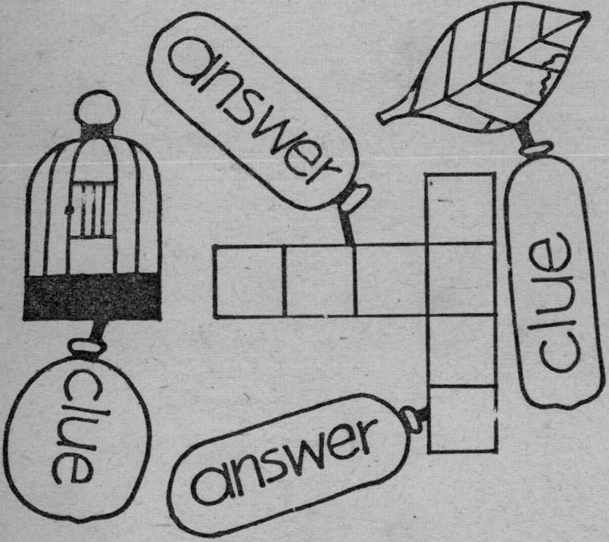

Puffin Books

This book is dedicated to Camilla Cavendish

Puffin Books, Penguin Books Ltd, Harmondsworth, Middlesex, England
Penguin Books, 625 Madison Avenue, New York, New York 10022, U.S.A.
Penguin Books Australia Ltd, Ringwood, Victoria, Australia
Penguin Books Canada Ltd, 2801 John Street, Markham, Ontario, Canada L3R 1B4
Penguin Books (N.Z.) Ltd, 182–190 Wairau Road, Auckland 10, New Zealand

First published 1977
Reprinted 1978

Made and printed in Great Britain by
Richard Clay (The Chaucer Press) Ltd
Bungay, Suffolk
Set in Monotype Univers

Contents

Words in Boxes

Look at these words and pictures. Find the right word for each picture.

Write the word in the boxes next to the picture. Write only one letter in each box.

We have put in one word for you. We have written it in big 'capital' letters. Always use **capital letters** in the boxes.

And always write with a **pencil** because pencil is easy to change if you make a mistake.

HAND SHOES WINDOW

BOX RABBIT SUN

Across and Down

Find the right words for the pictures, and fill in the boxes.

Some words go **across** →
as they did before. But
now some words go **down** ↓
too. We have put in one
down word for you.

CLOCK		P	T
		E	E
B	PIE	N	L
E		G	E
D		U	P
	SIX	I	H
		N	O
			N
			E

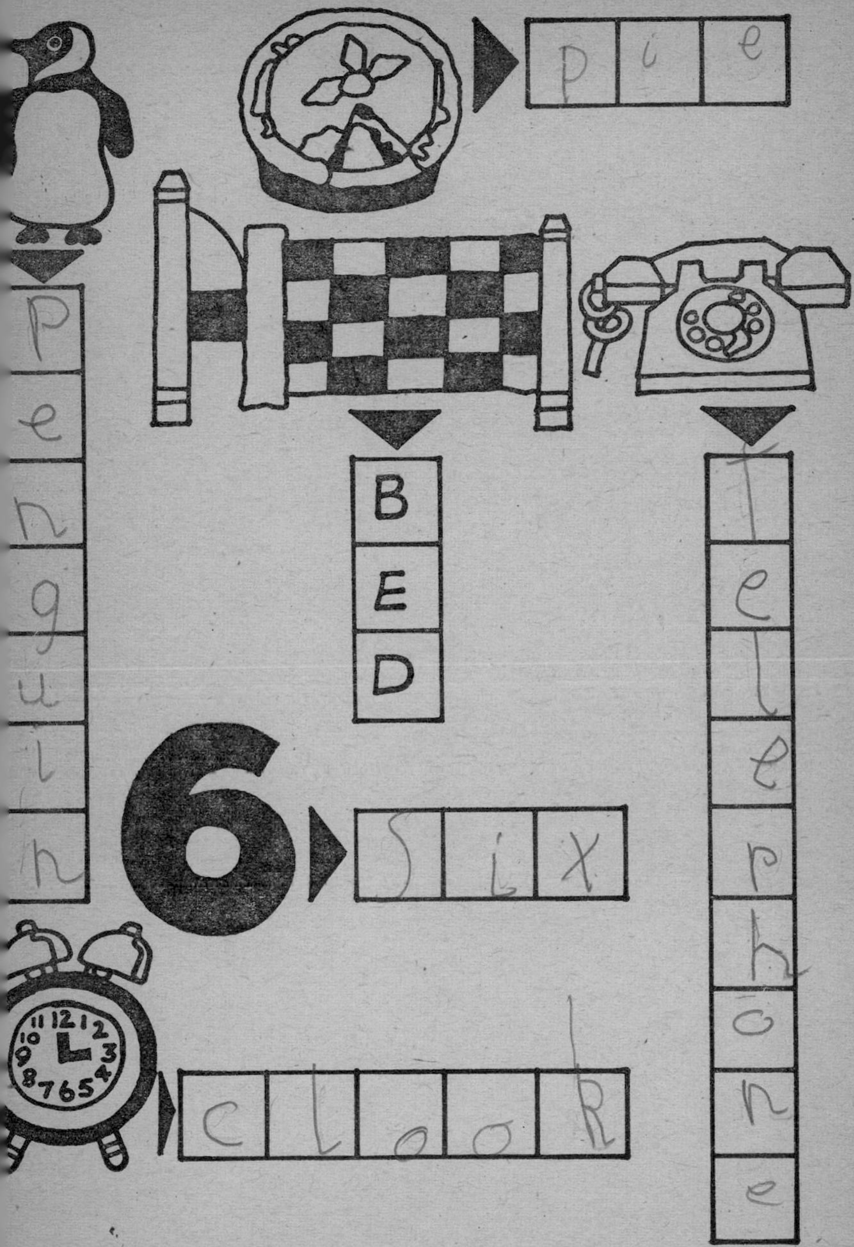
pie
penguin
BED
telephone
six
clook

Words that Cross

Here are the first real crosswords in this book. They are called **crosswords** because the **words cross** over each other.

Look at the first crossword. See how the P in SHIP is the same as the P in PIG. You write the P only once.

DOLL

HOUSE

SHIP

CAKE

PIG

CARROT

SHIP
PIG

> *Remember:*
> Write in big, capital letters.
> Use a pencil.

E
Y
E

UMBRELLA

S
A
W

M
O
N
E
Y

PIPE

NEEDLE

PENCIL

KITE

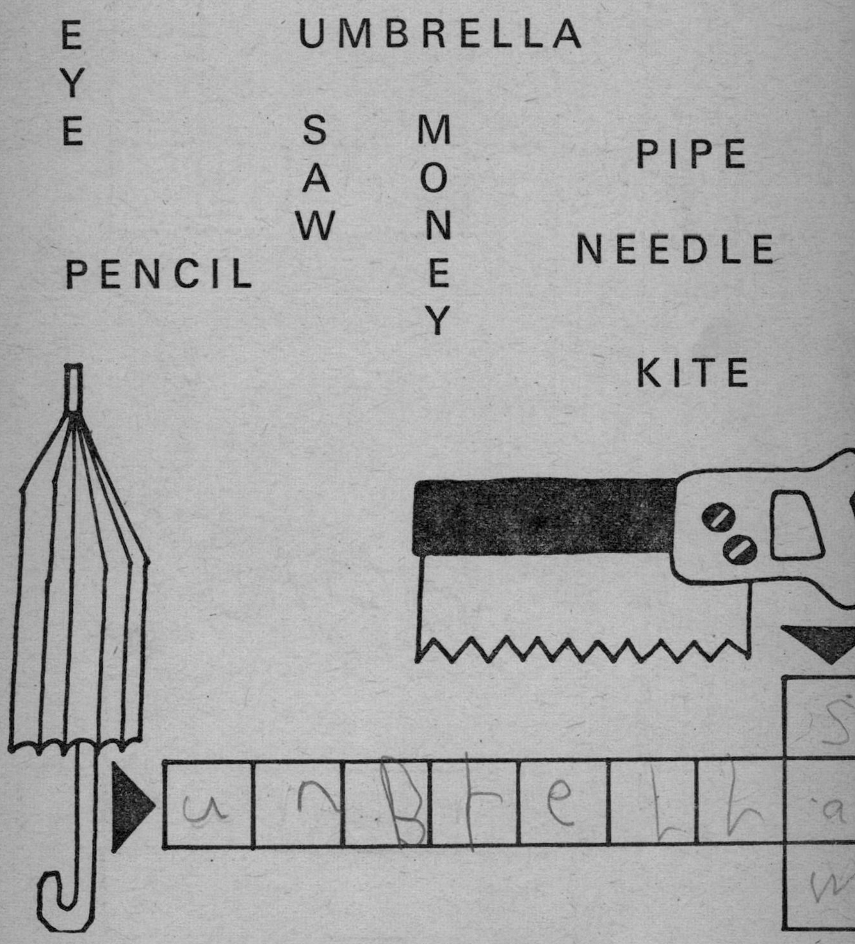

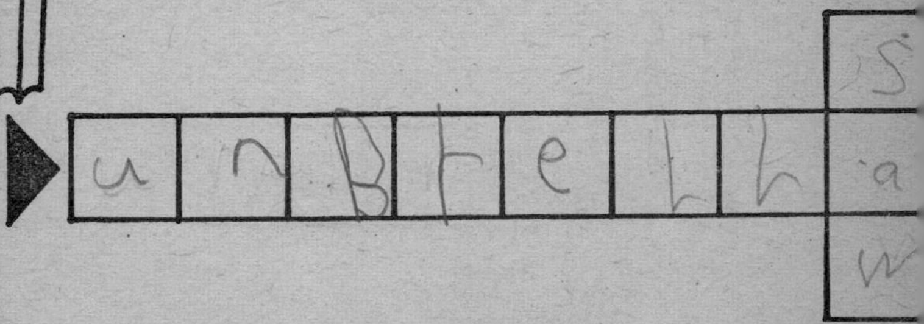

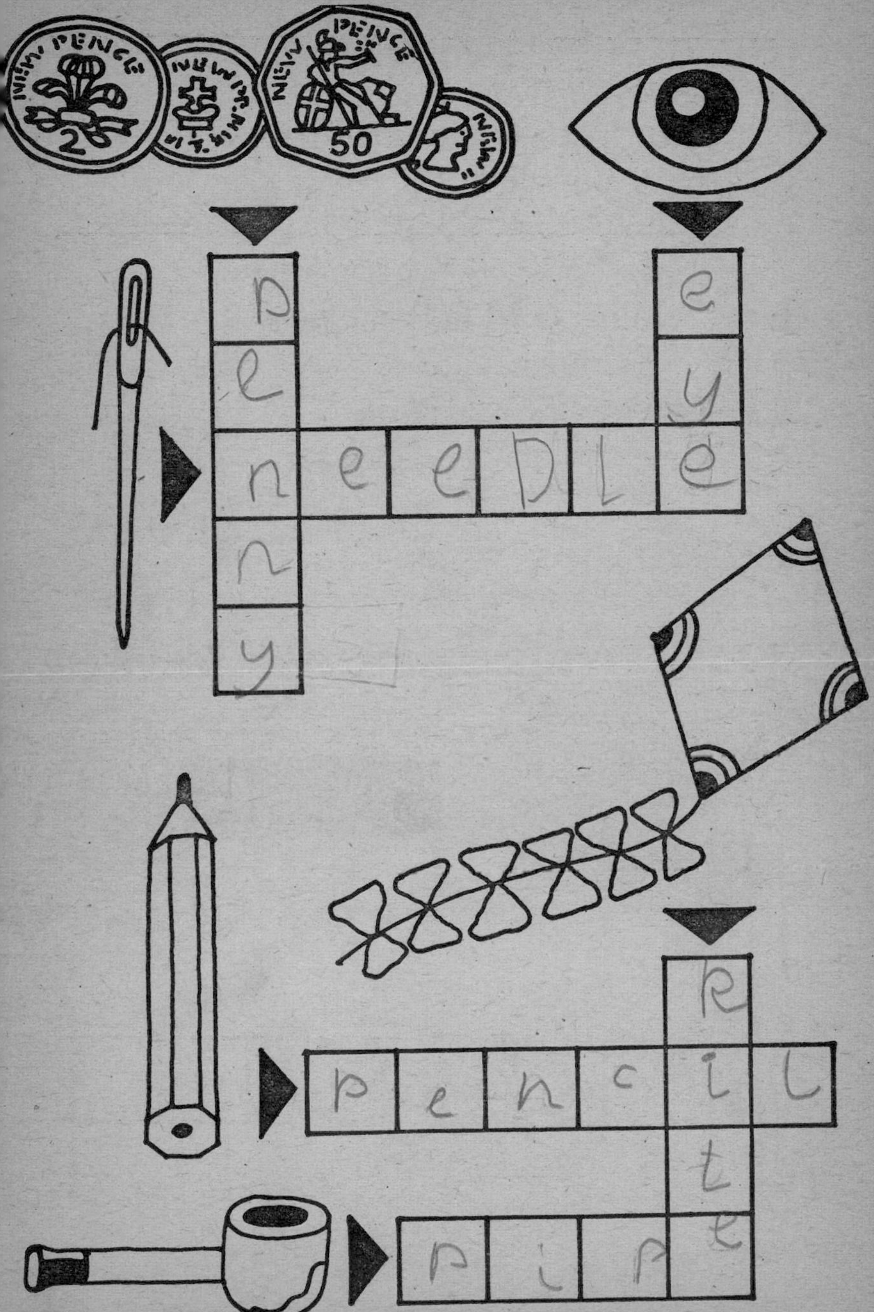
NEW PENCE
2
NEW PENCE
50

Clues and Answers

When we do crosswords the picture is called the **clue.** The word we write in the boxes is called the **answer.** Put CAGE and LEAF in the right boxes in the next crossword. Then look at what the balloons say.

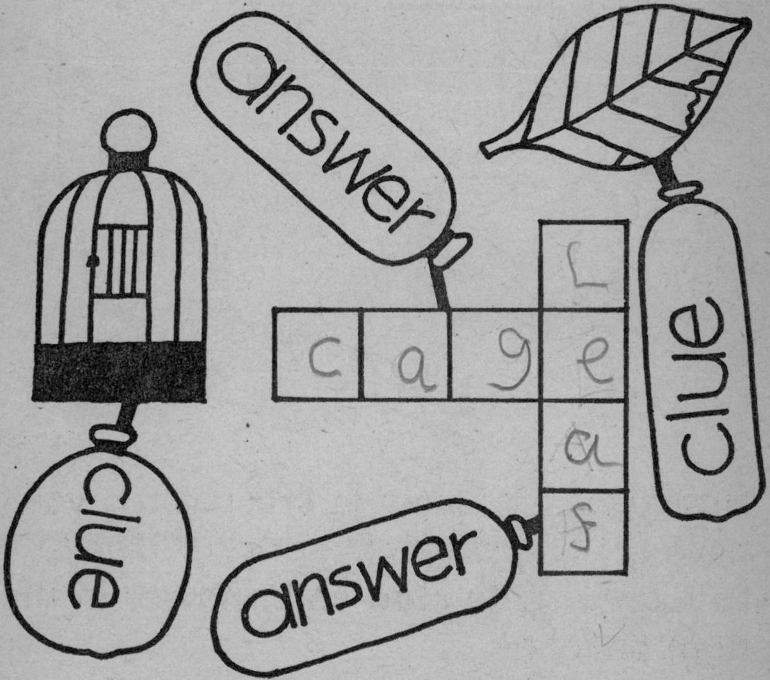

Put NEST and TOP in the right boxes in the next crossword. Then write **clue** or **answer** in the balloons.

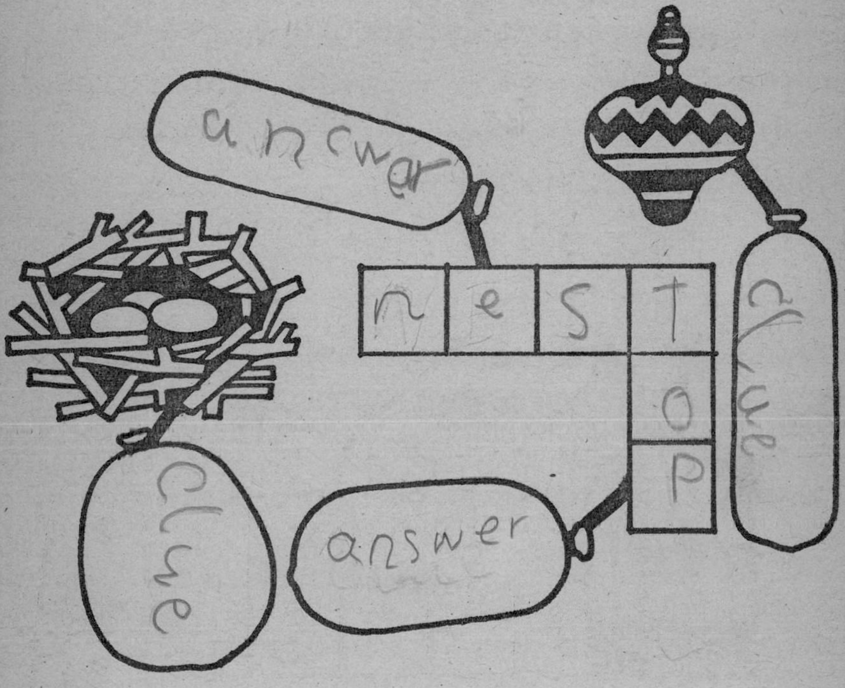

Now go back to some crosswords you have already done. Draw your own balloons. Write **clue** and **answer** in the right balloons.

More Words that Cross

As you can see there are no answers on the next page to help you.
But now every crossword has a special number, like this:

2

At the end of this book all the crosswords are shown with their special numbers, and with the answers written in. So you can look there if you really can't think of the right answers by yourself.

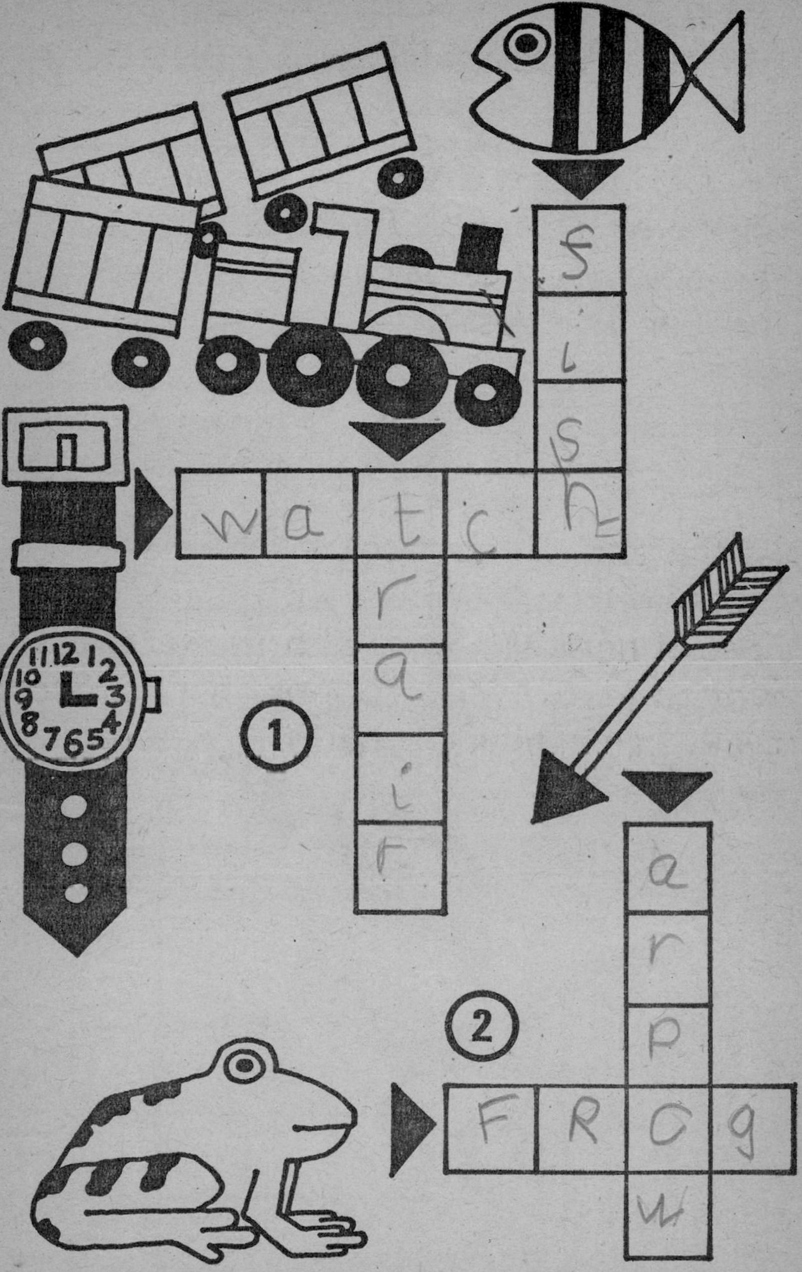
1
2

3

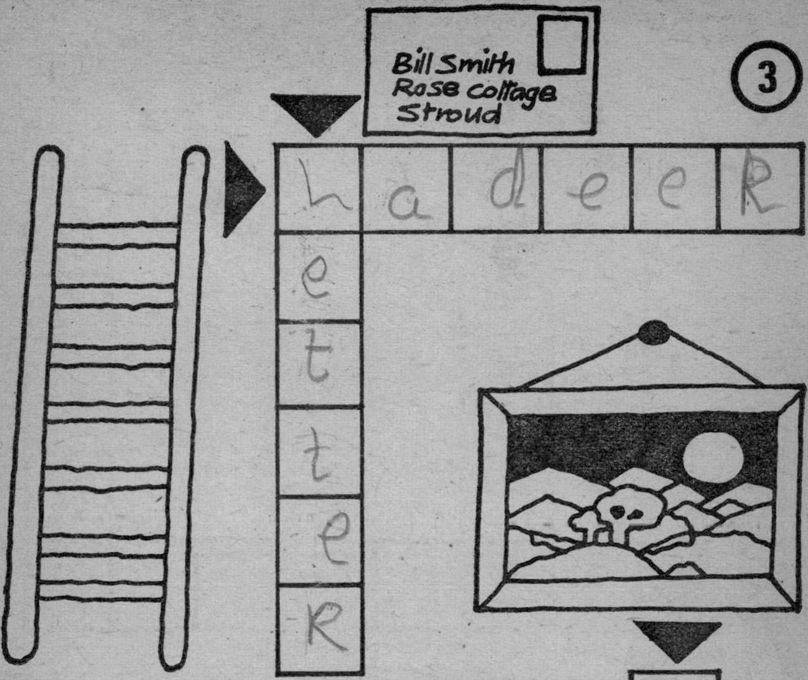
Bill Smith
Rose coltage
Stroud

4

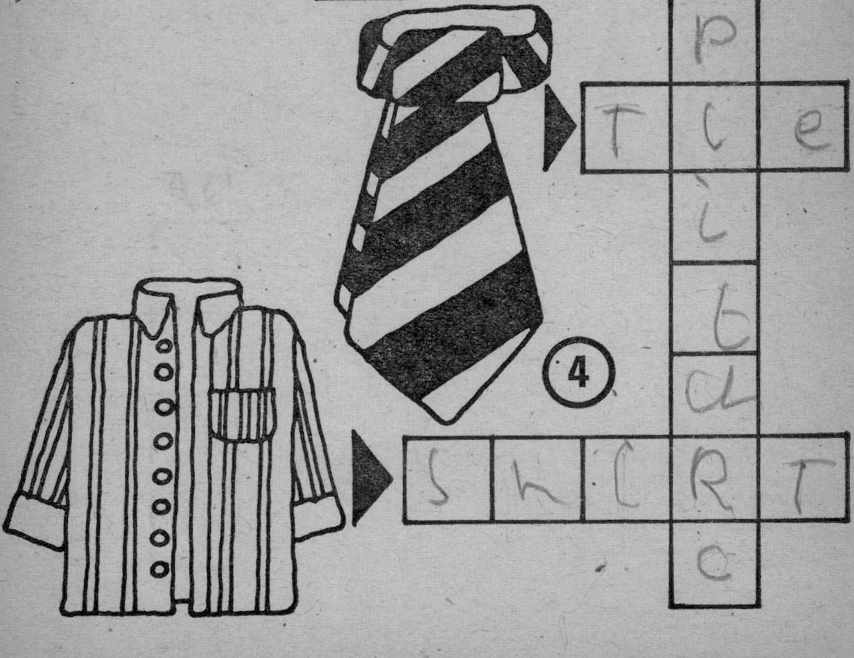

5

6

In a crossword, every word you can write helps you to guess another word.

So if you don't know the answer to one clue, go on and try other clues.

8
9

Black Boxes and Numbers for Clues

Look at the next crossword. Some of the boxes are black like this: ■ Of course you should never write in black boxes.

This crossword is a little one. It has only four words. But when a crossword has lots of words we can't fit in all the clues next to the answers. So we have to move the clues down under the crossword. We use numbers to help us. Look:

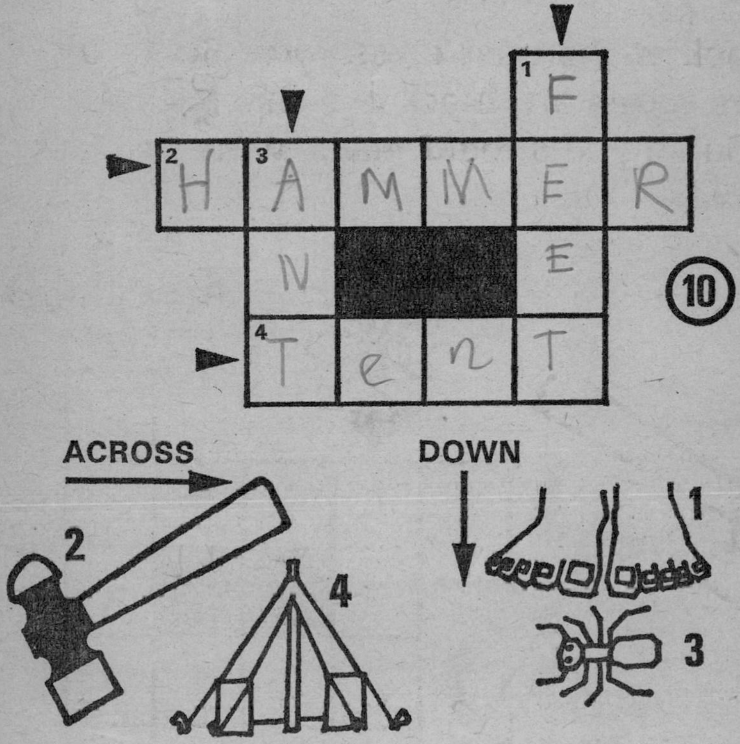

Each clue has a number. And the answer has the same number in the box where it starts. Clues for words that go **Across** ⟶ are in one list. **Down** ↓ clues are in a different list.

11

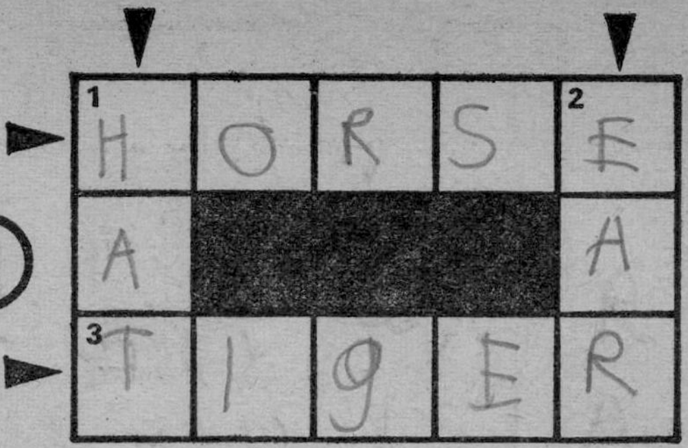

ACROSS → DOWN

12

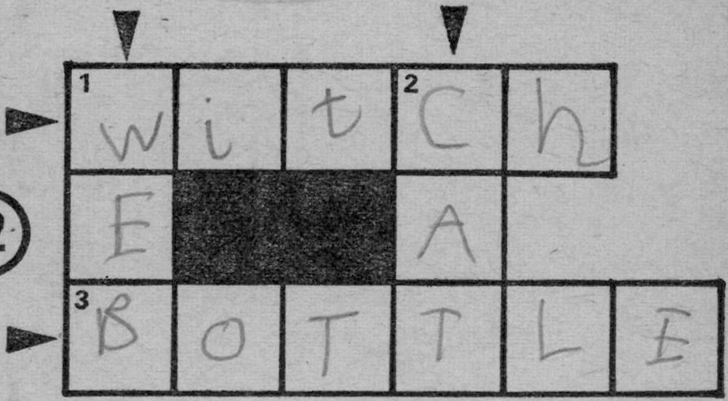

ACROSS → DOWN

13

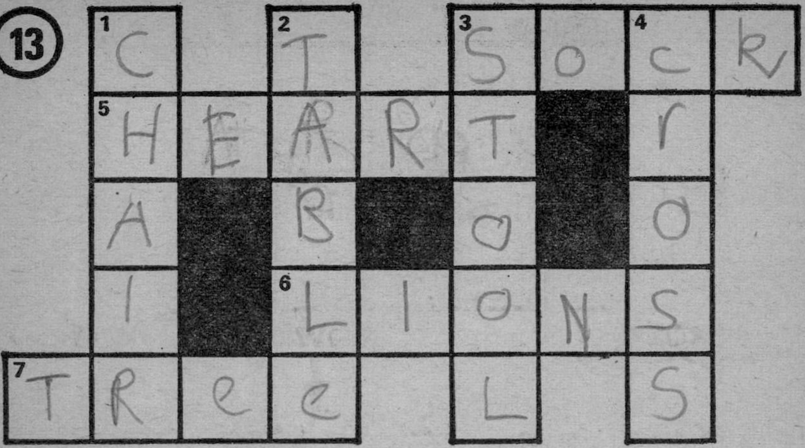

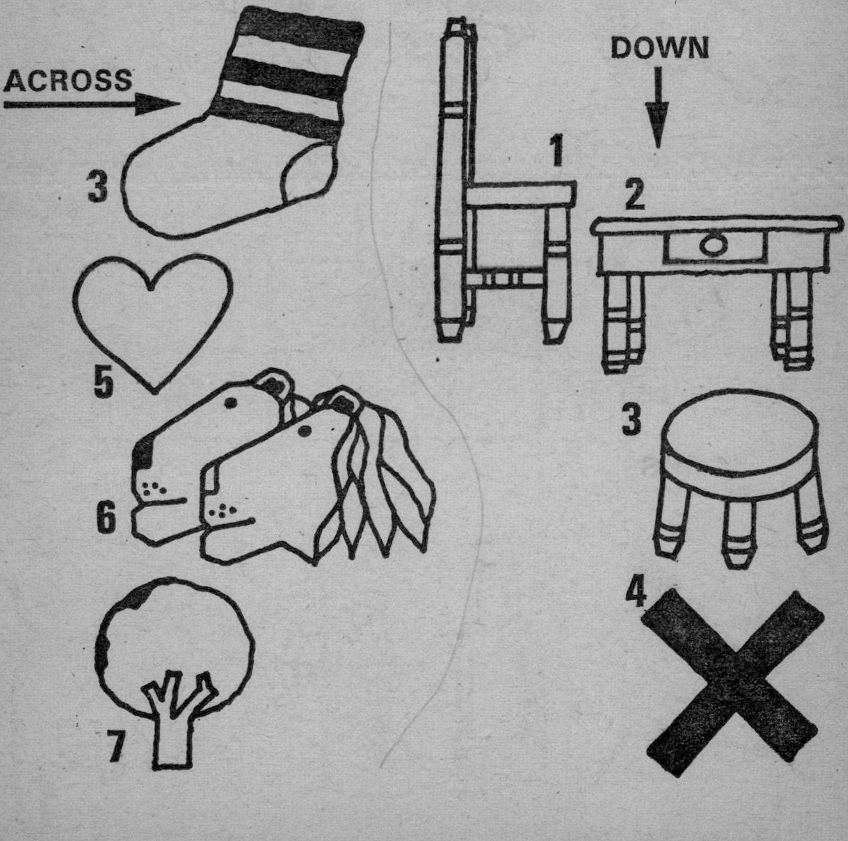

14

ACROSS →

DOWN ↓

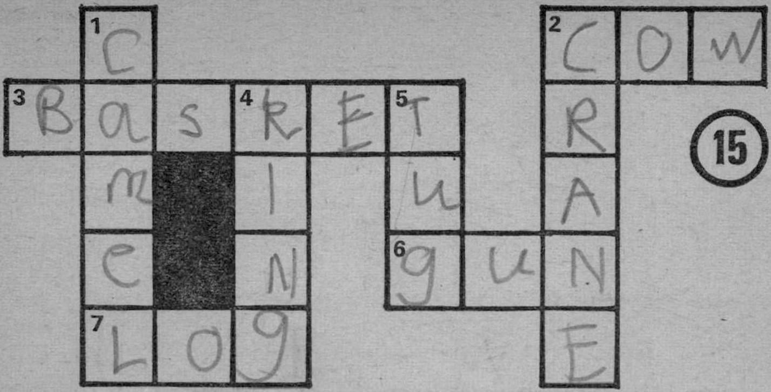

15

ACROSS

2

3

6

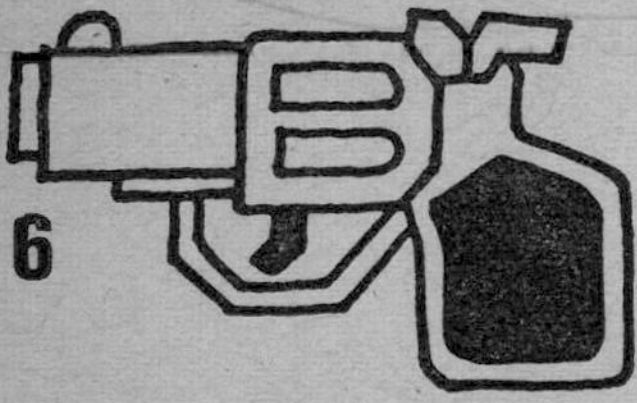

7

DOWN

1

2

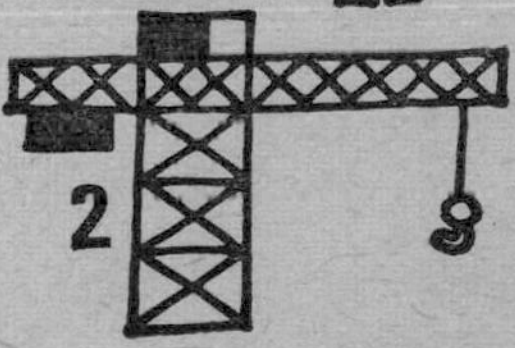

4

5

Words for Clues

Clues can't always be pictures. Think of the words BUT or NICE or ASK. Nobody can draw pictures of them.

When we want to use words like BUT in crosswords we have to write the clues in words too. The clues in adult crosswords are all in words.

In the next three crosswords the Down clues are in words. After that the Across clues are in words too.

16

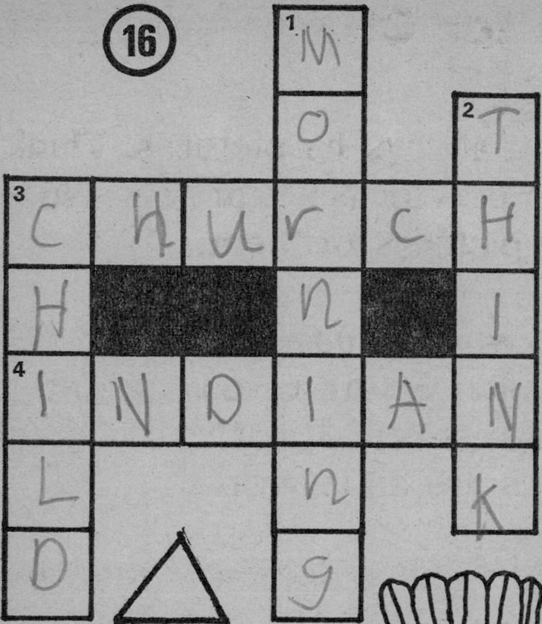

ACROSS

3

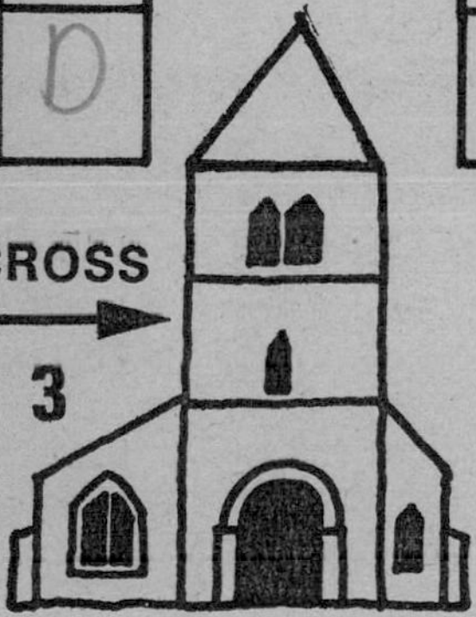

4

DOWN

1. The part of the day when you get up.
2. This word means something we do inside our heads. To spell it, take the A out of THANK and put an I in its place.
3. A person who is older than a baby and younger than a teen-ager.

17

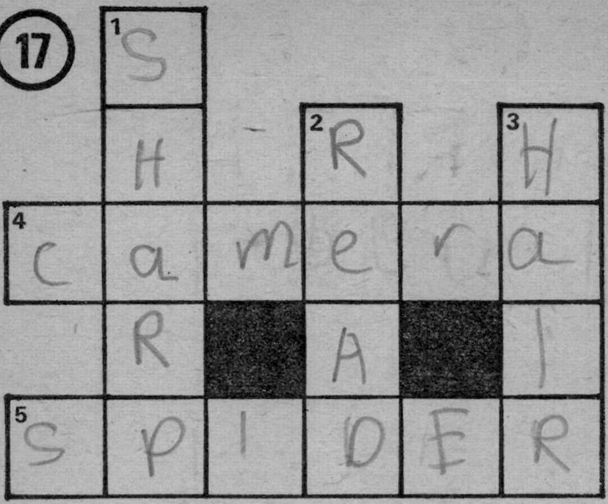

ACROSS

4

5

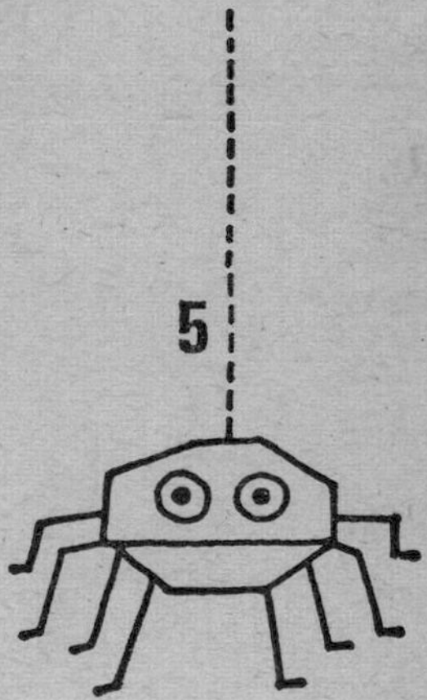

DOWN

1. If a knife is this you can cut yourself on it.
2. What you do when you look at the words in a book and say them out loud.
3. This grows on the top of your head.

18

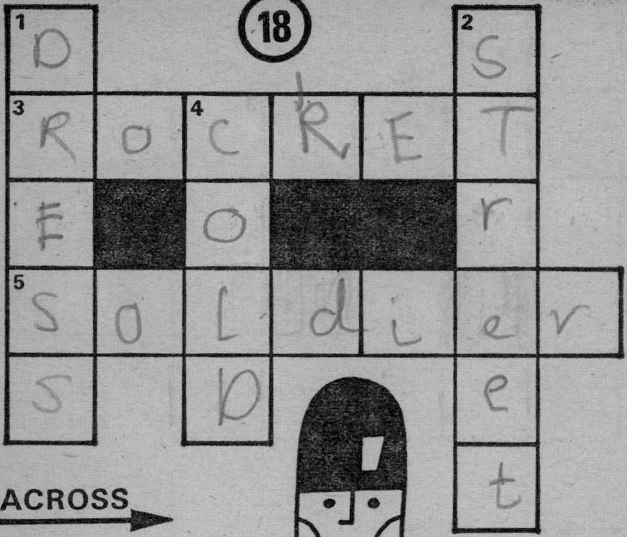

ACROSS

3

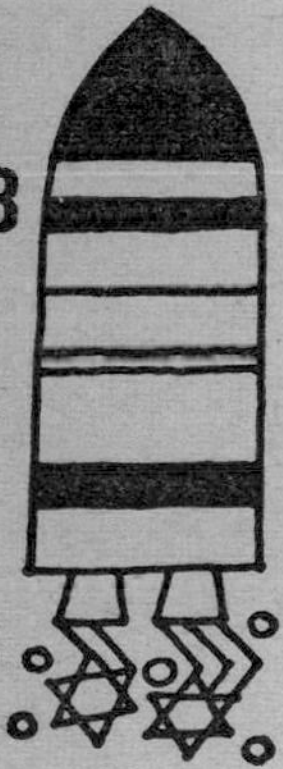

5

DOWN

1. What you do when you put your clothes on.
2. This is another word for a road.
4. If you catch this you will cough and sneeze.

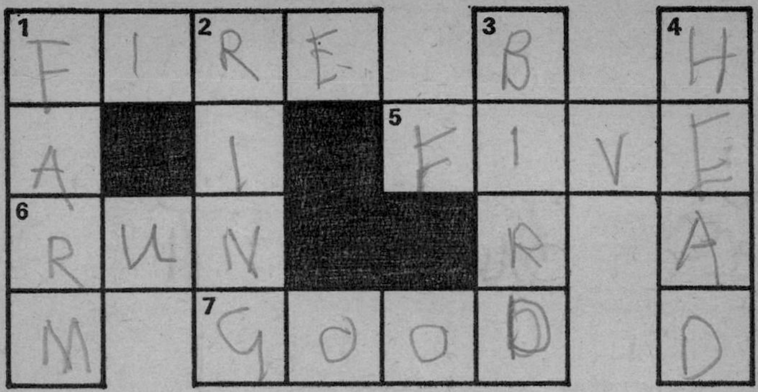

19

ACROSS

1. A fireman's job is to put this out.
5. Three and two make this number.
6. You do this when you are going as fast as you can.
7. If someone is kind and nice and always does the right thing we say he is this sort of person.

DOWN

1. A place with barns and fields and cows and sheep and pigs.
2. A round thing to wear around your finger.
3. It has a beak, wings and feathers.
4. What you have on top of your neck.

20

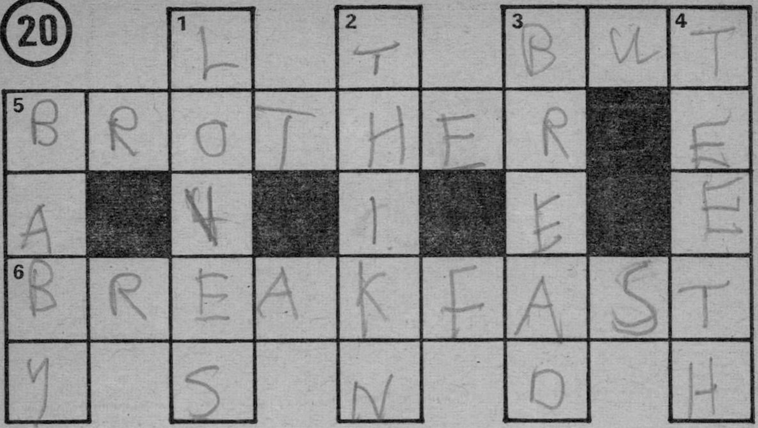

ACROSS

3. Write TUB backwards for this answer.
5. Mary is a SISTER to Tom. So what is Tom to Mary?
6. The first meal people eat in the morning.

DOWN

1. This word means 'likes very, very much .
2. If you do this with your head you mean NO.
3. You can toast this and butter it.
4. These shiny white things are in your mouth.
5. A very small, new person.

21

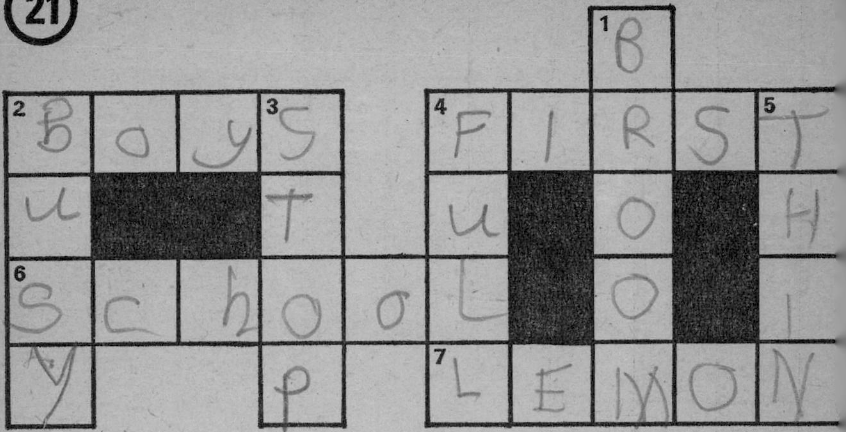

ACROSS

2. We call Sharon and Caroline GIRLS. What do we call Andrew and John?
4. It comes before SECOND and THIRD.
6. A place with classes and teachers.
7. A yellow fruit with a sour taste.

DOWN

1. People sweep with it and a witch is supposed to ride on it.
2. We are this when we are working hard.
3. Write POTS backwards to get this answer.
4. How you feel when you have eaten plenty.
5. We can be sure that this sort of person is not FAT.

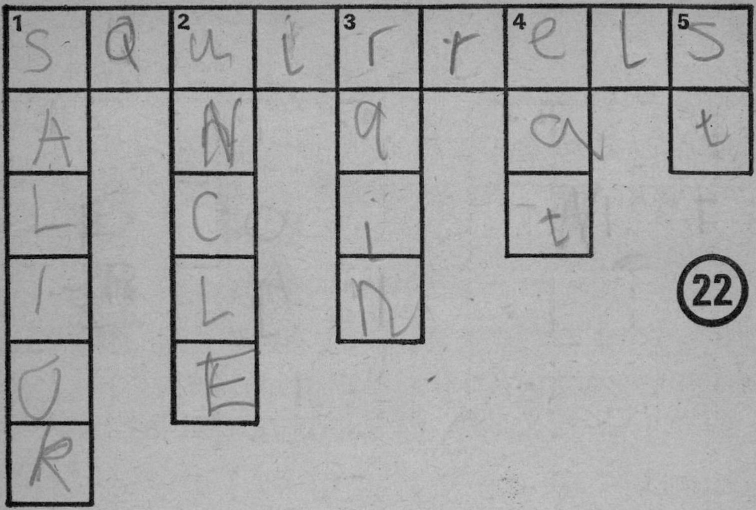

22

ACROSS

1. They have bushy tails, they live in trees, and they love to eat nuts.

DOWN

1. He works on a ship.
2. He is married to an AUNT.
3. Water that falls from the sky.
4. We DRINK milk. What do we do with bread?
5. A short way to write STREET.

Opposites

Sometimes a clue will ask you to find the **opposite** of a word.

Opposites are words which mean things so different that they can never both be true at the same time. Your LEFT hand can't be your RIGHT hand. The TOP of a tree can't be the BOTTOM of the tree.

Can you find the opposites of these words?

DOWN	⟷	u	p	
GOOD	⟷	B	a	D
COLD	⟷	H	o	t

Answers

UP, BAD, HOT

23

ACROSS

2. The opposite of PUSHES.
5. The opposite of AFTER.
6. When two countries fight each other, what is the fight called?
7. The opposite of BACK.
9. The opposite of GO SLOWLY.
10. Something we sing.

DOWN

1. The opposite of RICH.
2. A small coin.
3. The opposite of HIGH.
4. This comes after WINTER and before SUMMER.
5. A sandy place by the sea.
7. The thick hair a cat has all over its body.
8. The opposite of YES.

24

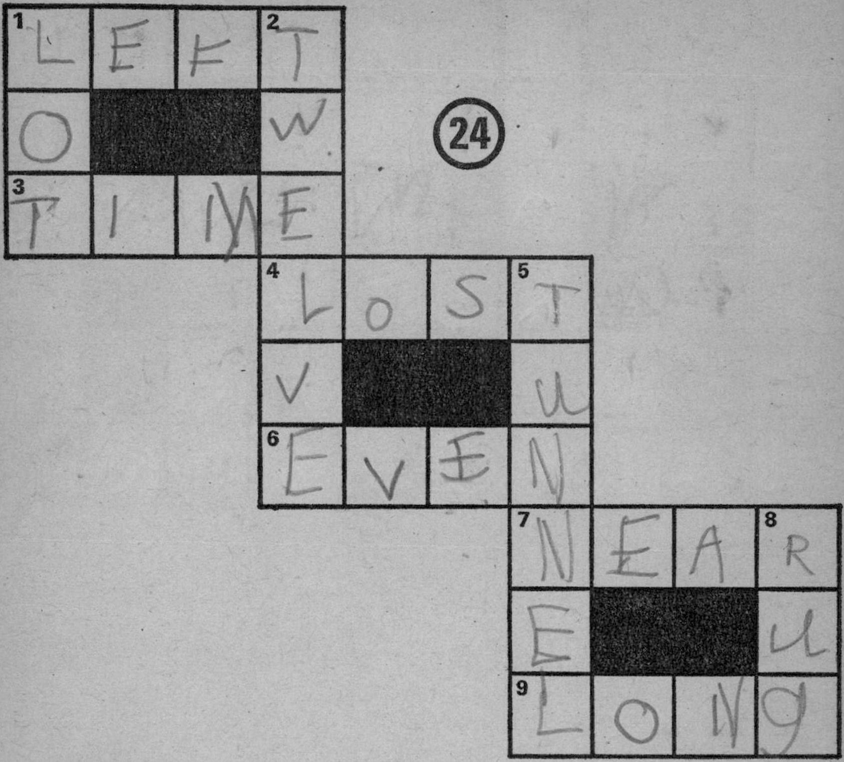

ACROSS

1. One of your feet is your RIGHT and the other is this.
3. What a clock tells.
4. A thing is this if you can't find it.
6. This word means 'smooth'. You can find it among the letters of SEVENTY.
7. The opposite of FAR AWAY.
9. The opposite of SHORT.

DOWN

1. You can find this little word in PLOTTING and also in SHALLOT.
2. Add five and seven for this answer.
5. When a train goes under a hill it runs through this.
8. A small carpet.

25

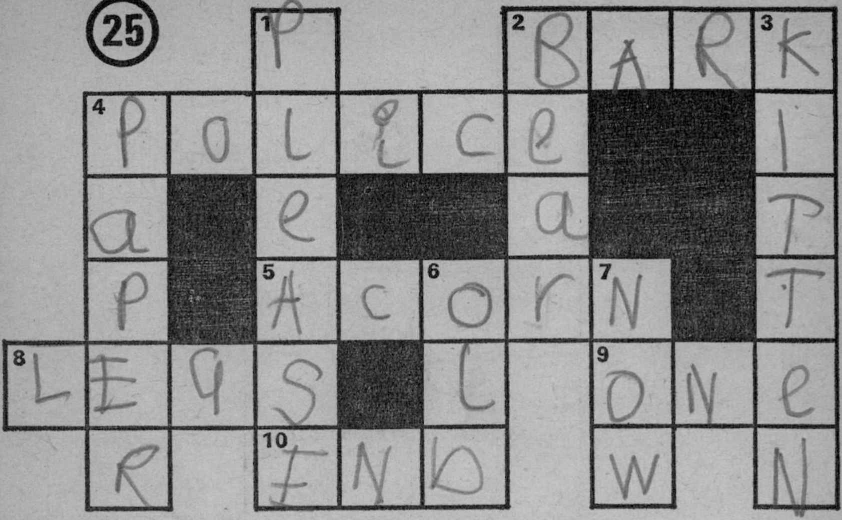

ACROSS

2. A loud noise that a dog makes.
4. Their job is to catch crooks and robbers.
5. A nut from an oak tree.
8. We walk with these.
9. The number that comes before TWO.
10. The opposite of BEGIN.

DOWN

1. It is polite to say this when we ask for something.
2. Yogi or Teddy or Paddington.
3. A baby cat.
4. This page is made of it.
6. The opposite of YOUNG.
7. This word means 'at this time'.

Lost Words

Sometimes a clue will look like this:

'Jack and – – – – went up the hill'

The little lines mean that a word has been left out. The answer to the clue is the lost word. This time of course it is JILL. (The number of lines is the same as the number of letters in the lost word.)

Can you find the lost words in these clues?

'Baa, baa black sheep, have you any – – – –?'

'We – – – – – Kings of Orient are.'

– – – – Poppins

Answers

WOOL, THREE, MARY

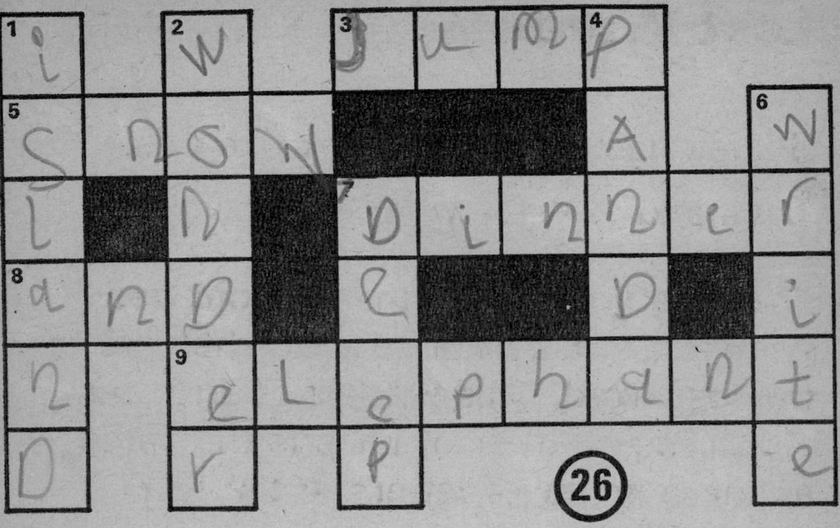

ACROSS

3. 'Hop, skip and – – – –.'
5. '– – – – – White and the Seven Dwarfs.
7. Your biggest meal of the day.
8. 'Bedknobs – – – Broomsticks.'
9. It has tusks and a long trunk.

DOWN

1. A piece of land with sea all around it.
2. 'Twinkle twinkle little star, how I – – – – – – what you are.'
4. A black and white animal from China which looks very like a bear.
6. You do this when you put words on to paper.
7. 'When the snow lay round about, – – – – and crisp and even.'

A Colour Puzzle

27

ACROSS

2. The colour of wood.
4. Grass is this colour.
5. The colour of night.
6. If you have a lot of this you are rich.
8. The colour of snow.
10. You could mix red and blue paint to get this colour.
12. This pale red is also the name of a beautiful garden flower.

DOWN

1. A buttercup is this colour.
3. This bright colour is also the name of a fruit.
6. Mix black and white for the colour of an elephant.
7. Many coins are this colour.
9. The colour of the sky.
11. This colour says STOP!

28

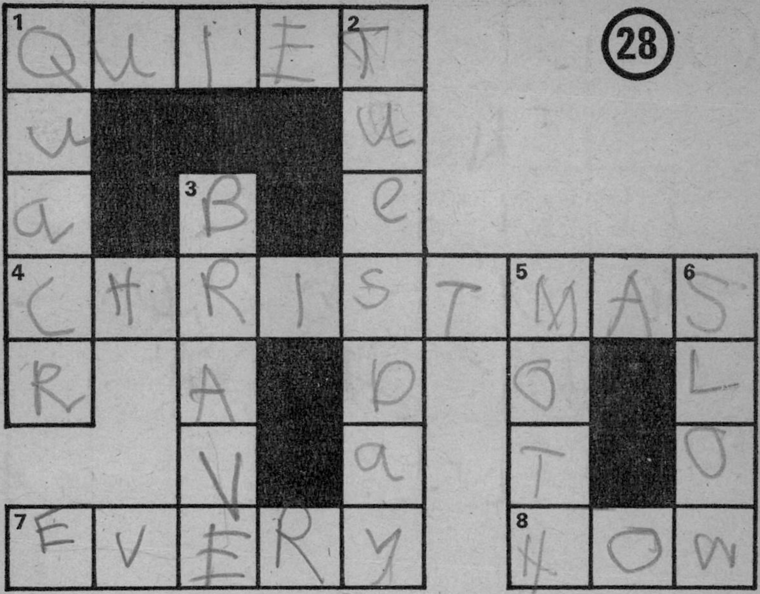

ACROSS

1. The opposite of NOISY.
4. A special day in December when we have a tree and give presents.
7. 'Mary had a little lamb, its fleece was white as snow, and – – – – – where that Mary went that lamb was sure to go.'
8. What lost word goes on the lines in these questions: '– – – much does it cost?' '– – – old are you?'

DOWN

1. The noise a duck makes.
2. The day after Monday.
3. A Red Indian warrior. This word also means 'without fear'.
5. It is like a butterfly but it flies at night.
6. The opposite of FAST.

29

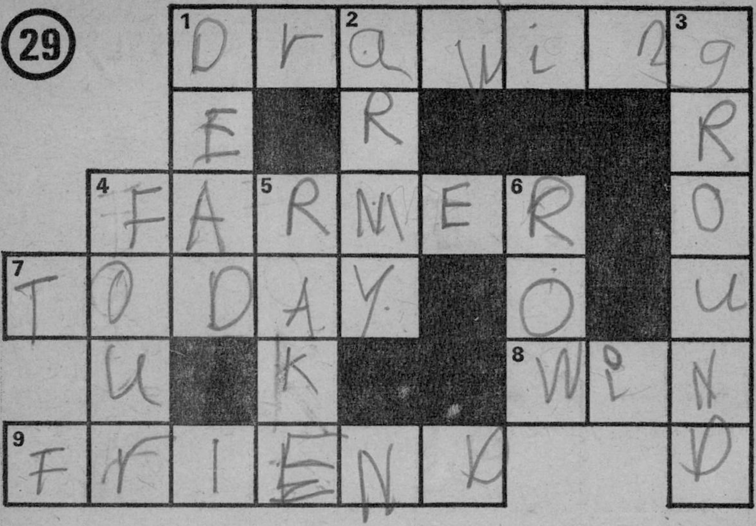

ACROSS

1. A picture made with a pencil.
4. He owns a farm.
7. What comes between YESTERDAY and TOMORROW?
8. To come in first in a race.
9. Someone you like and who likes you.

DOWN

1. The opposite of ALIVE.
2. Soldiers belong to it.
3. Inside your home you stand on the FLOOR. What do you stand on outside?
4. Two and two.
5. A garden tool like a big comb with a long handle.
6. What people do with oars to make a boat move.

Anagrams

Look at these words:

OWLS SLOW

They are both made from the same letters — L, O, S and W. So we say that OWLS is an **anagram** of SLOW. And SLOW is an **anagram** of OWLS.

When a clue tells you to find the anagram of a word, try to think of the letters mixed up in different ways. You might think 'OWLS — WOLS — LOWS — SWOL — SLOW!'

Or you can write the letters down and keep mixing them until you guess the right word.

Can you find the answers to these clues?

1. NET is an anagram of a number. What is the number?

T	E	N

2. Find the anagram of ART which means a nasty animal a bit like a mouse.

R	A	T

3. Find the anagram of POT which means the opposite of BOTTOM.

T	O	P

4. END is an anagram of the home of a lion. What is this home called?

D	E	N

5. LUMP is an anagram of the name of a fruit. What is the fruit?

P	L	U	M

Answers

1. TEN, 2. RAT, 3. TOP, 4. DEN, 5. PLUM

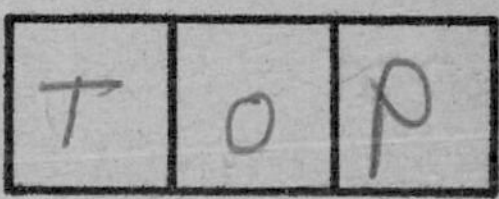

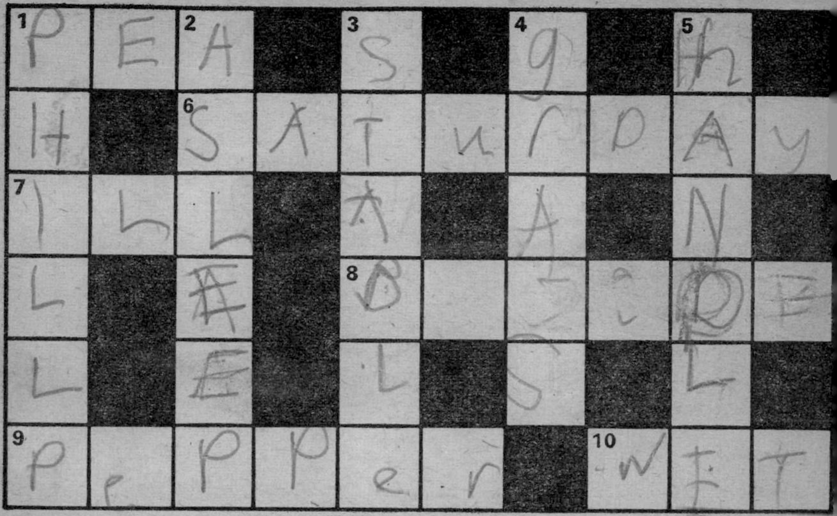

30

ACROSS

1. APE is an anagram for this little green vegetable.
6. The day after Friday.
7. Take FRY out of FRILLY. The letters you have left spell a word that means 'not well'.
8. SEE BID is an anagram for a word that means 'next to'.
9. People keep this on the table with the salt.
10. The opposite of DRY.

DOWN

1. A boy's name. Its anagram is HIP LIP.
2. At night most people are this in bed.
3. BLEATS is an anagram for the house of a large farm animal.
4. Green stuff that grows on lawns.
5. A door has this to help you open it.

31

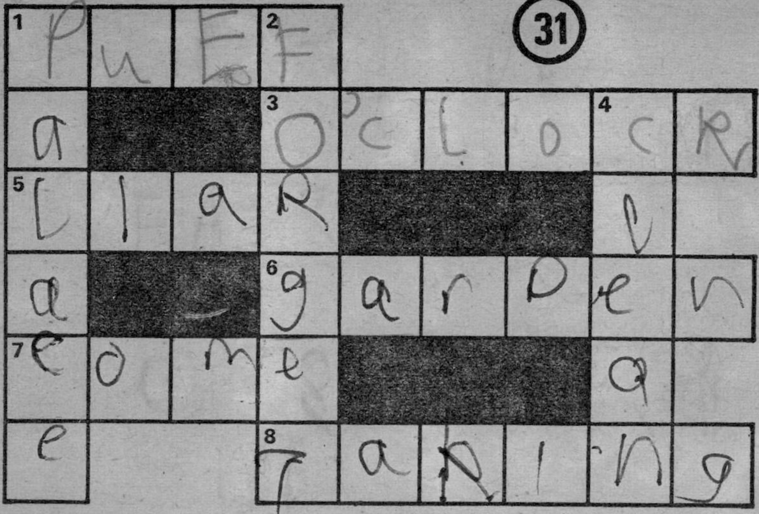

ACROSS

1. 'I'll huff and I'll – – – – and I'll blow your house down.'
3. When the long hand on a clock points to the 12 and the short hand points to the 5, it is five – – – – – – – .
5. RAIL is an anagram for this person who doesn't tell the truth.
6. A place with grass and flowerbeds around a house.
7. The opposite of GO AWAY.
8. Cross the L out of TALKING to spell this answer.

DOWN

1. A building where a king and queen live.
2. The opposite of REMEMBER.
4. The opposite of DIRTY.

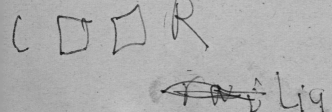

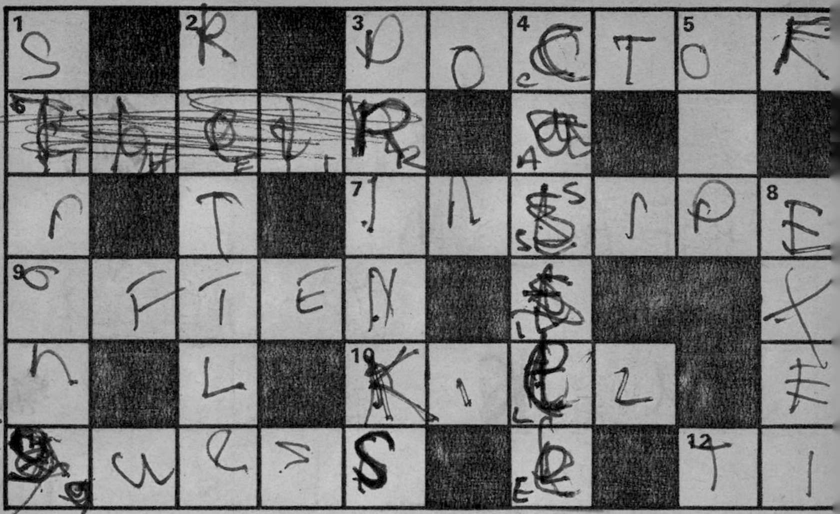

32

ACROSS

3. When we are not well he helps to make us better.
6. Babies can't put – – – – – own clothes on.
7. The opposite of OUTSIDE.
9. Find the anagram of NO EFT which means 'many times'.
10. This word means to make dead.
11. What you do to find an answer when you don't really know it.
12. Take STING out of SITTING to find this little word.

DOWN

1. The opposite of WEAK.
2. This has a spout and a handle and we keep it specially for boiling water.
3. Meat, fruit and vegetables are FOODS. What are water, coffee and Coca-Cola?
4. A big building with a drawbridge.
5. 2 and 4 are EVEN numbers. What kind of a number is 3?
8. You come in through the ENTRANCE and go out through the – – – –.

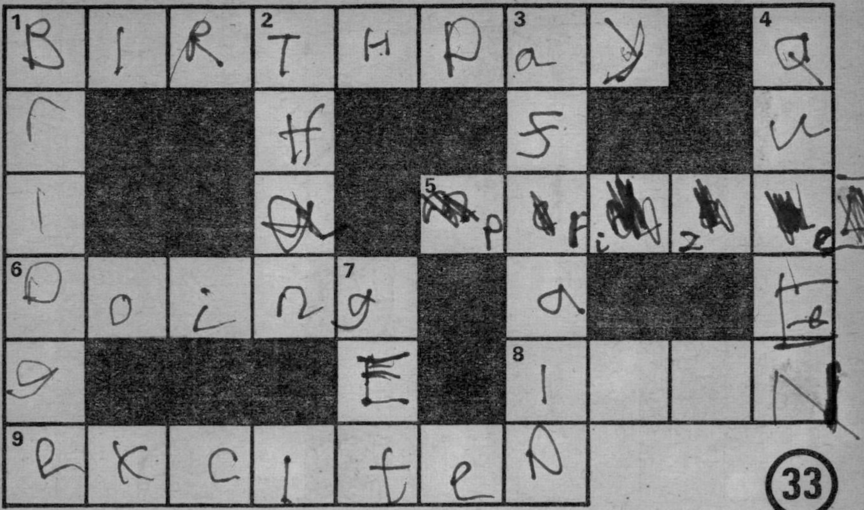

33

ACROSS

1. This is the day you were born, and you get presents on it every year.
5. A special present given to a winner.
6. This word means 'making' or 'being busy'. Its anagram is DIG ON.
8. Mother uses this to make clothes smooth and dry.
9. Upset but happy, the way you may feel before a party.

DOWN

1. People build this over a river so that they can cross from one side to the other.
2. 'Five is bigger – – – – four.'
3. AIR FAD is an anagram for how we feel if we are frightened.
4. She is the mother of a prince.
7. This word is hiding in TARGET and in TOGETHER and in FORGET. What is it?

Twelve Months Make a Year

34

ACROSS

4. This month comes between July and September.
5. The first three letters of the last month.
7. PETER MEBS is an anagram of this month.
8. Find the month hidden in the letters of this sentence: THE ISLAND OF CAPRI LOOKS BEAUTIFUL.
11. This month begins with New Year's Day.
12. Put together the beginning of JUNGLE and the end of BUBBLY to spell this month.

DOWN

1. This month comes before December.
2. The only month that begins with O.
3. The sixth month.
6. The second month.
9. 'Here we go gathering nuts in – – – .
10. CHARM is an anagram of this month.

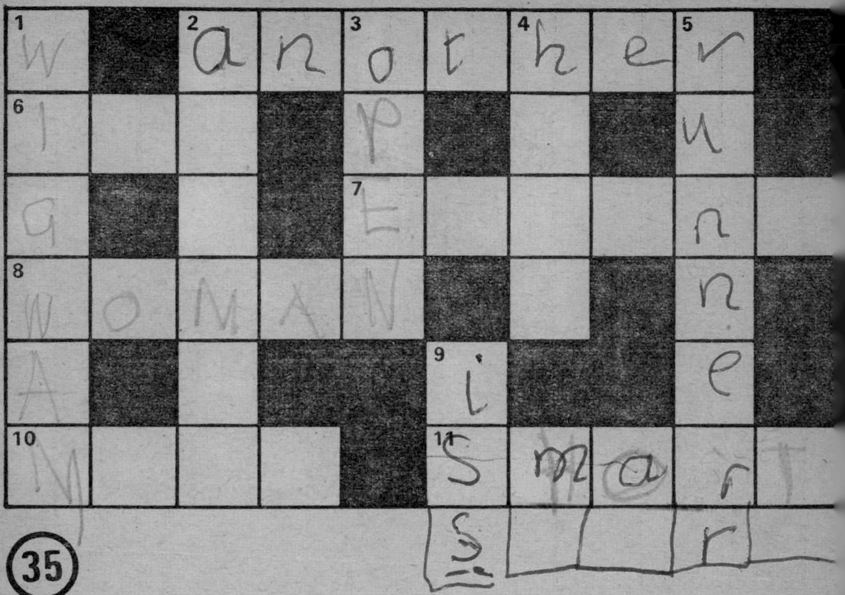

35

ACROSS

2. 'Rain, rain, go away, Come again – – – – – – – – day.'
6. A boy's name. You can find it among the letters of INDIANA.
7. It pulls a train, or makes a car go.
8. If Peter is a MAN, what is Anne?
10. A white drink that cows make for us.
11. The opposite of TALL.

DOWN

1. Some Red Indians lived in this kind of tent.
2. This is alive and not a plant. MANILA is an anagram of it.
3. The opposite of SHUT.
4. The opposite of LOW.
5. A person who runs.
9. 'London Bridge – – falling down.'

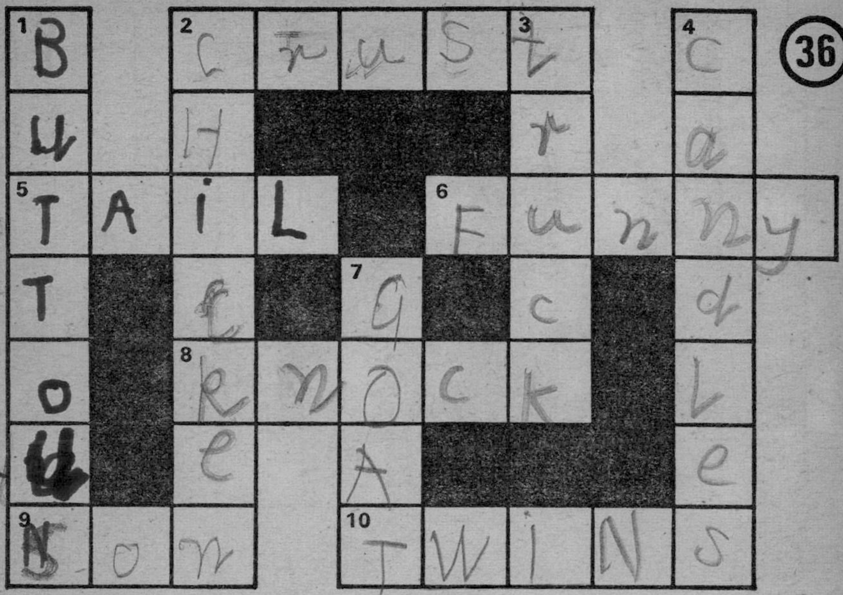

36

ACROSS

2. Bread has this on the outside.
5. A dog wags it when he is happy.
6. If something is this it makes you laugh.
8. To hit on a door with your knuckles.
9. Carol is Michael's MOTHER, so Michael must be Carol's – – – .
10. These two children look the same, and have the same parents, and were born on the same day.

DOWN

1. They go through buttonholes.
2. A hen's baby.
3. A big vehicle. It rhymes with STUCK.
4. They are lit on a birthday cake.
7. A farm animal with horns and a beard.

The Empty Box Game

Here are two words that cross. But one box is empty. Can you guess what letter should go in it?

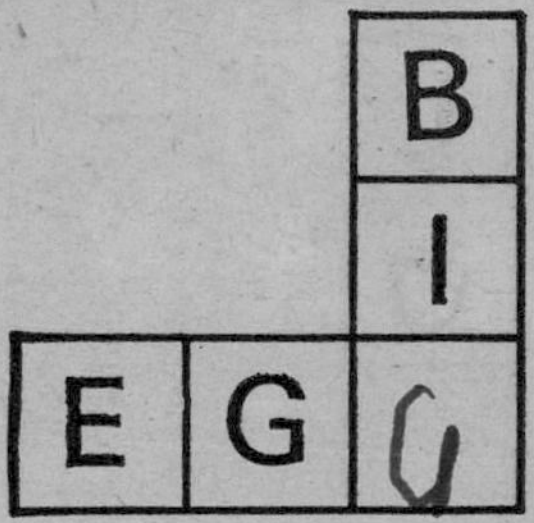

Remember, you must make a word both ways. If you put a T in the box the Down word would be BIT but the Across one would be EGT, which isn't a word at all. Of course the right letter in this puzzle is G.

Try to guess what letters go in the empty boxes on the next three pages.

37

Z E B R A
O
O

38

F
O
M I X

39

B
A F T E R
C
K

40

L
O
O
M A R K E T

41

D
O
O W L
N

42

A L W A Y S
I
G
N

43

H
U
C O _ I C S
P

44

UICK

U
E
E

ADIO

45

F
A
C Y
M

46

W
H
DA

47

C
R
O

F
U

I D

48

L
P SH
C
S Y
Y

49

W
A T
S O
T U
T
NORT

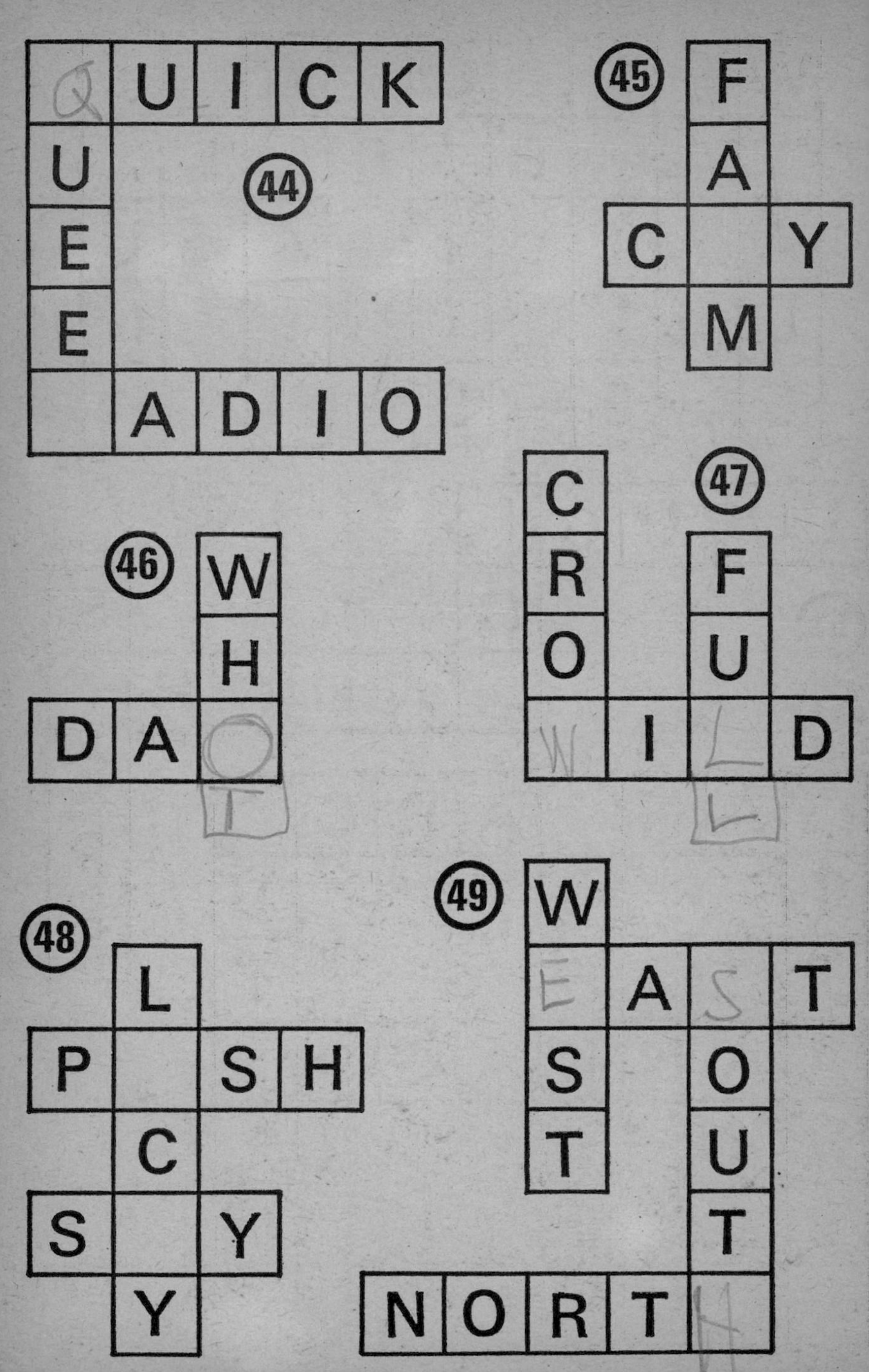

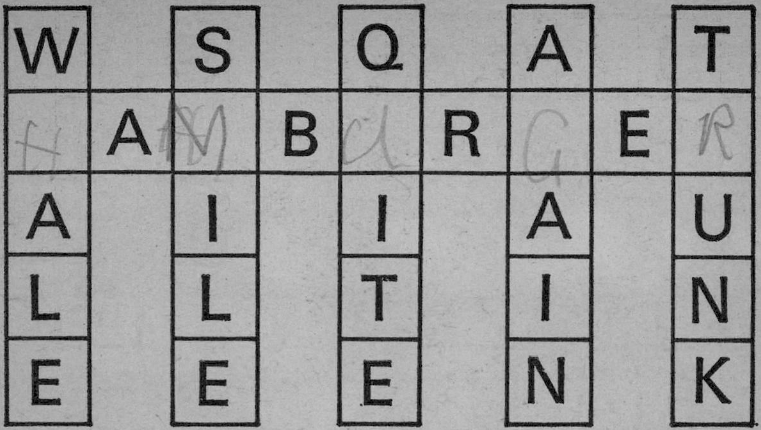

W S Q A T
A B R E
A I I A U
L L T I N
E E E N K

50

L A U G
O
S
A U G H
E
P
S

51

52

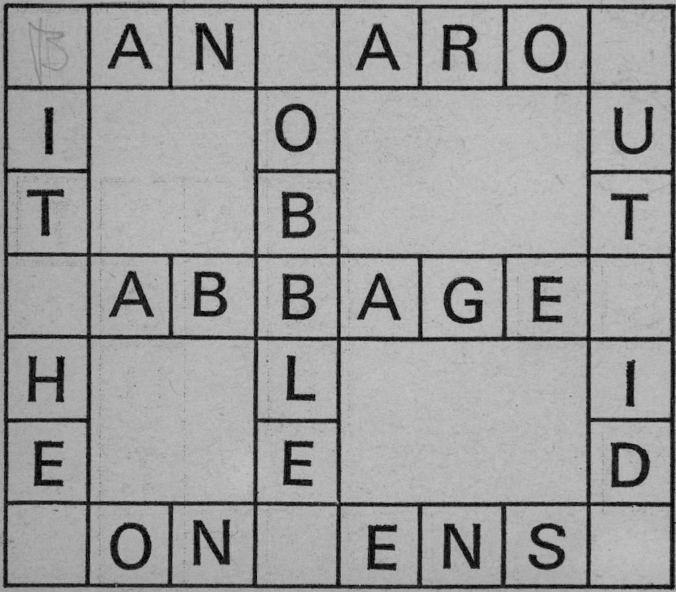

A N A R O
I O U
T B T
A B B A G E
H L I
E E D
O N E N S

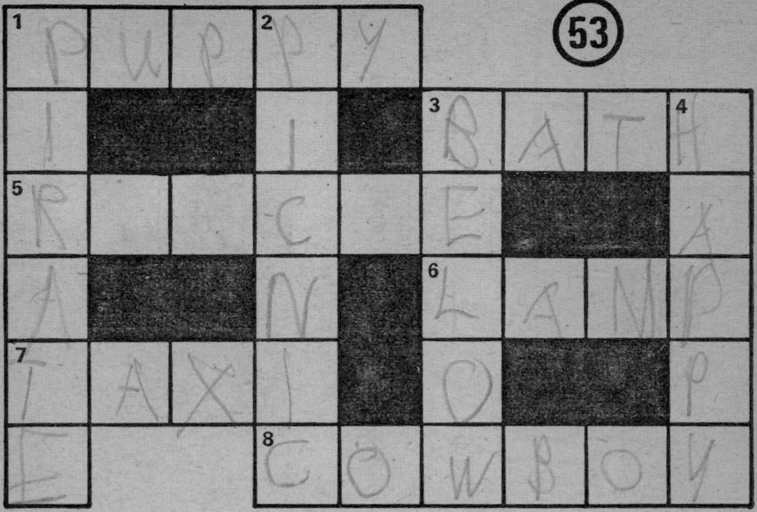

53

ACROSS

1. A baby dog.
3. You wash your whole body in this.
5. If you save someone from danger you do this to them.
6. The kind of light that stands on a table.
7. You pay the driver of this special car to take you where you want to go.
8. A man who rides on a horse and looks after cattle.

DOWN

1. His flag is the skull-and-crossbones.
2. A meal you take with you and eat out in the country.
3. The opposite of ABOVE.
4. The opposite of SAD.

54

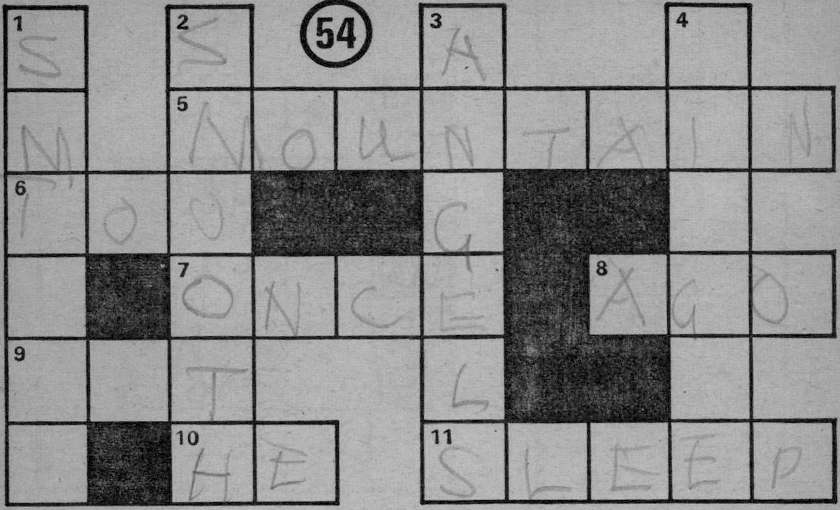

ACROSS

5. This is like a hill, but very, very much bigger.
6. 'Sea water is much – – – salty for us to drink.'
7. ' – – – – upon a time.'
8. 'It happened a long, long time – – – .'
9. This word means 'allow'. It is hidden in the letters of PIGLET and also in LETTUCE.
10. SHE means a woman. What word like SHE means a man?
11. This goes on a bed under a blanket.

DOWN

1. The opposite of BIG.
2. The opposite of ROUGH.
3. 'Hark the herald – – – – – – – sing.'
4. ' – – – – – – – bells, – – – – – – – bells, – – – – – – – all the way.'

A Very Big Breakfast

55

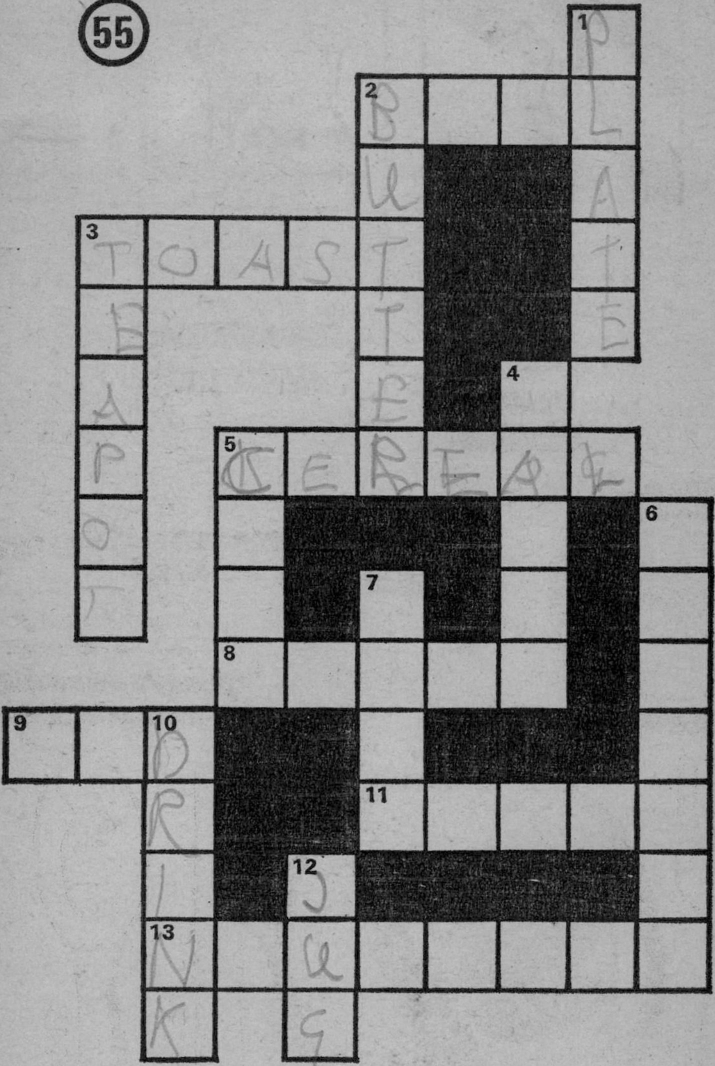

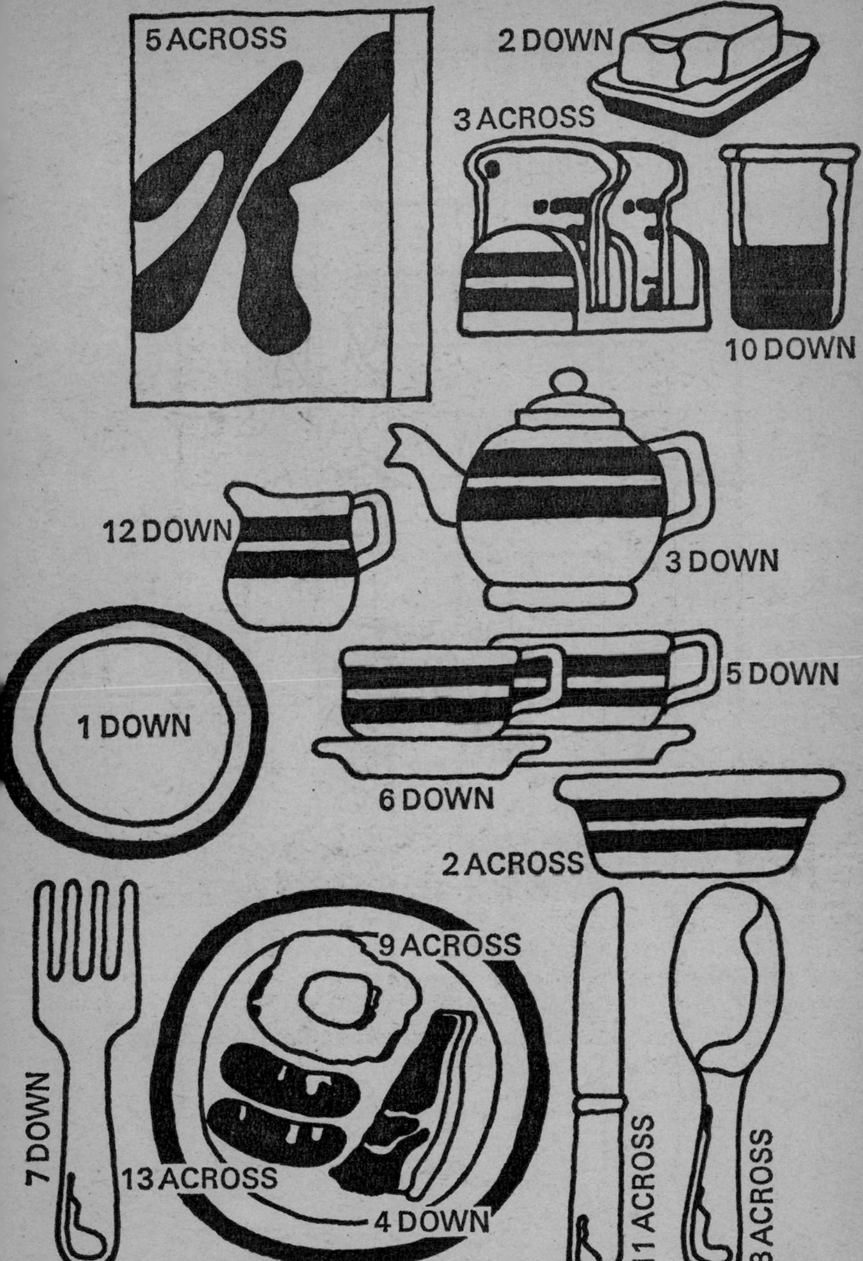
5 ACROSS
2 DOWN
3 ACROSS
10 DOWN
12 DOWN
3 DOWN
1 DOWN
5 DOWN
6 DOWN
2 ACROSS
9 ACROSS
7 DOWN
13 ACROSS
4 DOWN
11 ACROSS
8 ACROSS

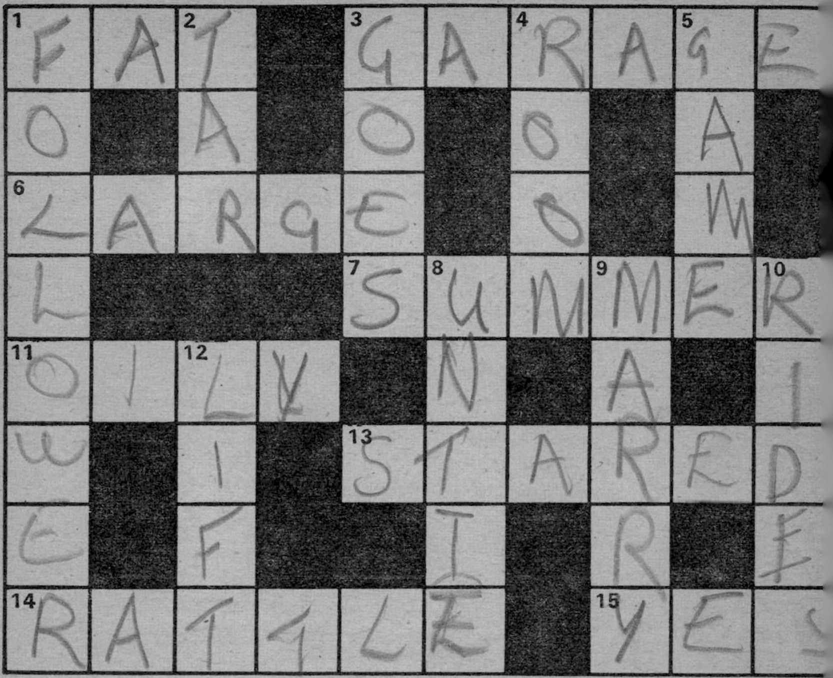

56

ACROSS

1. The opposite of THIN.
3. A house for a car.
6. ELGAR is an anagram of this word, which means 'big'.
7. The hottest part of the year.
11. This word means 'greasy'.
13. Looked at something hard for a long time, and rudely.
14. A noisy toy for a baby to shake.
15. The opposite of NO.

DOWN

1. A person who follows.
2. RAT is an anagram of this black sticky stuff. It is often spread on roads.
3. 'Rings on her fingers and bells on her toes, She shall have music wherever she – – – – .'
4. What is the anagram of MOOR which means a place in a house?
5. Something we play, like football or Rummy or Monopoly.
8. UNITE is an anagram of what we do to a knot to open it out.
9. When a bride and groom go to church this is what they are going to do.
10. A person does this when he travels on a horse.
12. This word means to raise something up.

Trace and Fit

This is a game like a crossword back-wards. We show you the shape of the crossword. And we give you the words. But can you fit the words in the right places on the shape?

This is how you do it. Suppose we give you a shape like this:

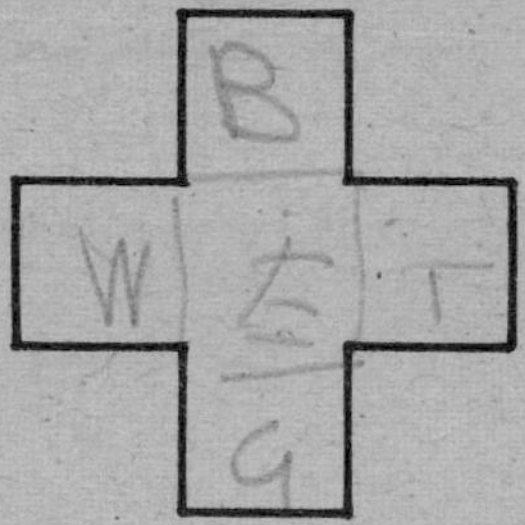

and words like these:

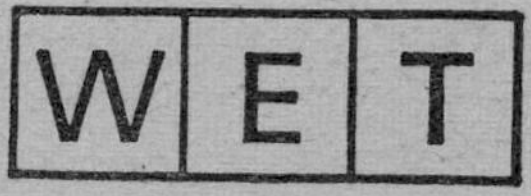

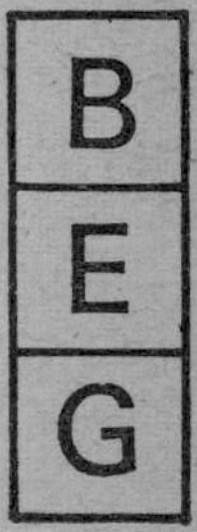

You trace the words on to a piece of paper, and cut them out. Then you look for a letter which is the same in both words. This time it is E. So you put one E on top of the other E to make the words fit in the shape, like this:

B
WET
G

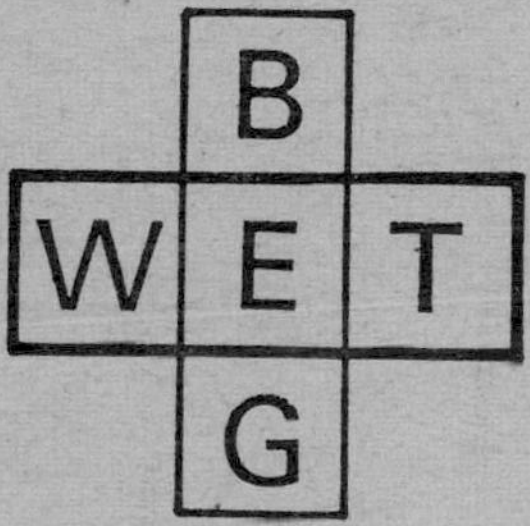

If you are quite sure that nobody else will want to use this book, you can cut out the words instead of tracing them. But first do the crossword on page 72!

WAX

TAN

DOT

OUT

SET

NUT

TIP

PAT

TIN

RECORD

KNIGHT

RIG

CAT

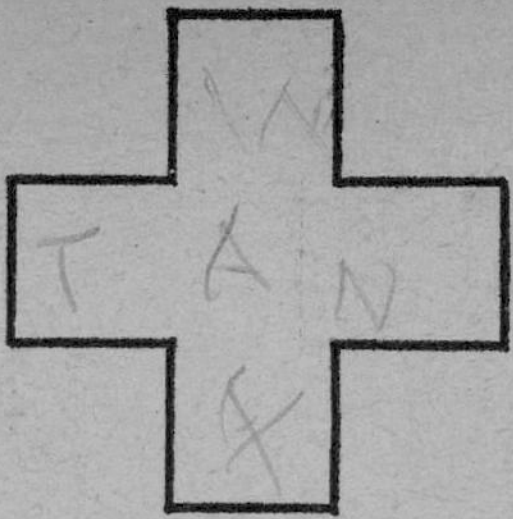

57

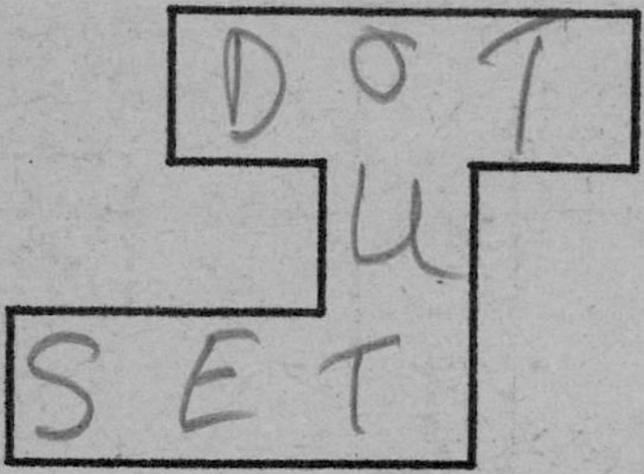

58

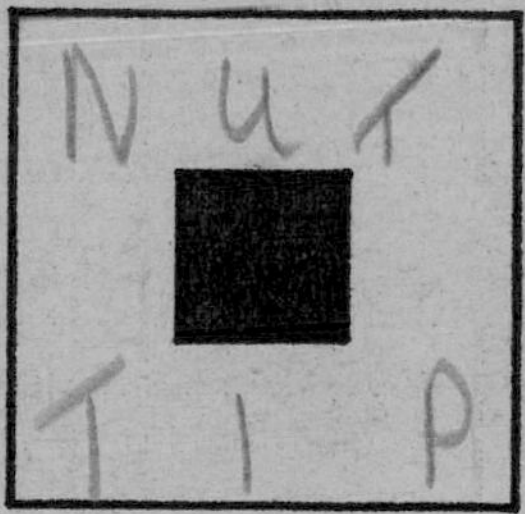

59

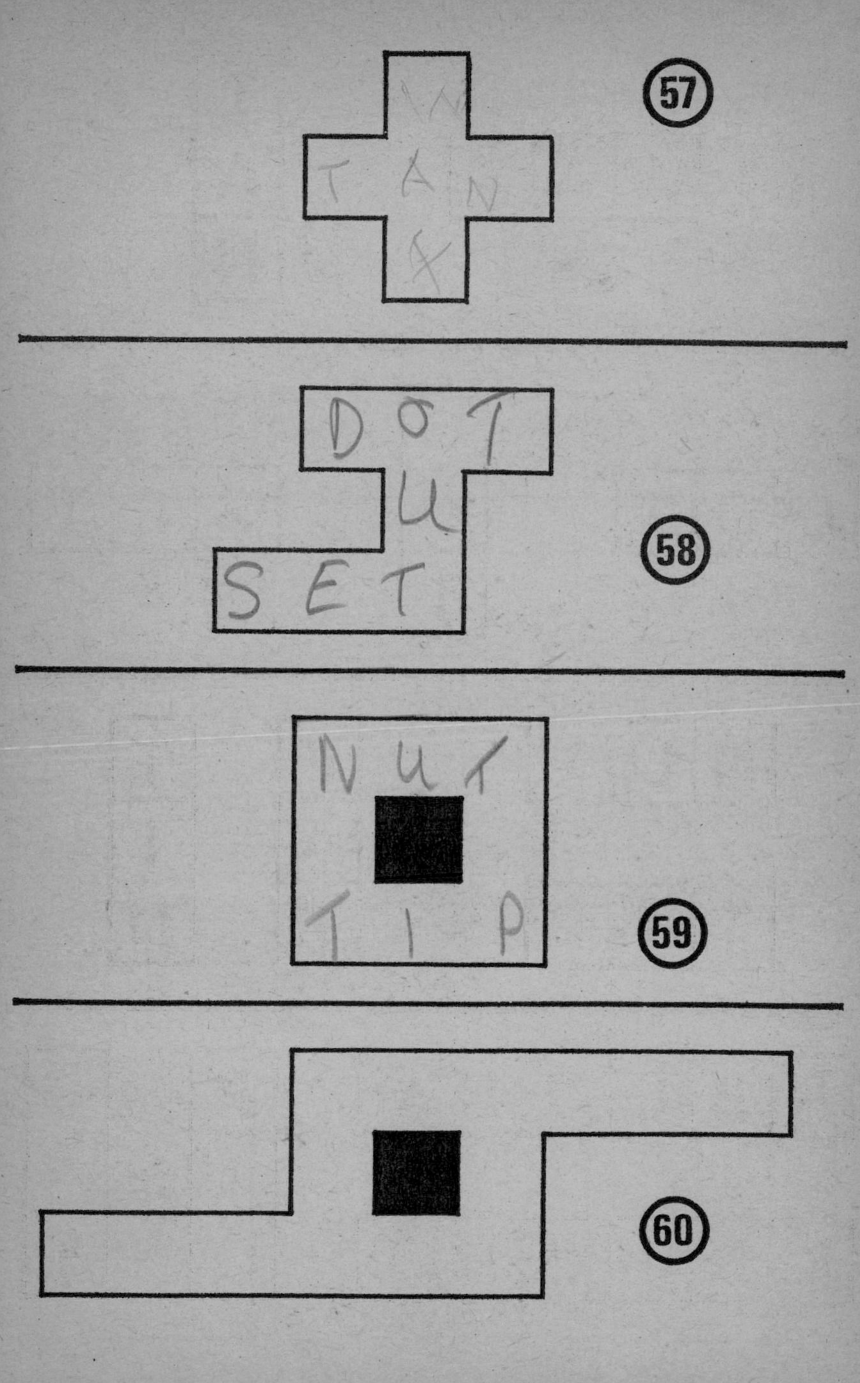

60

61

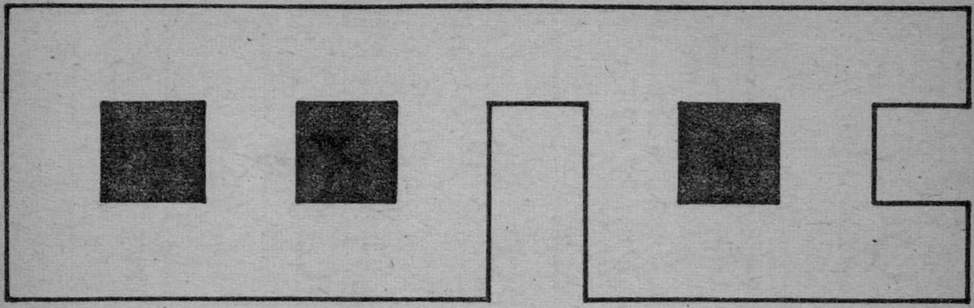

62

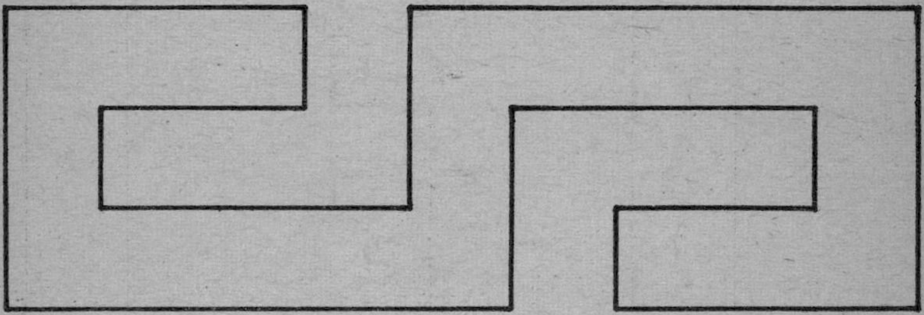

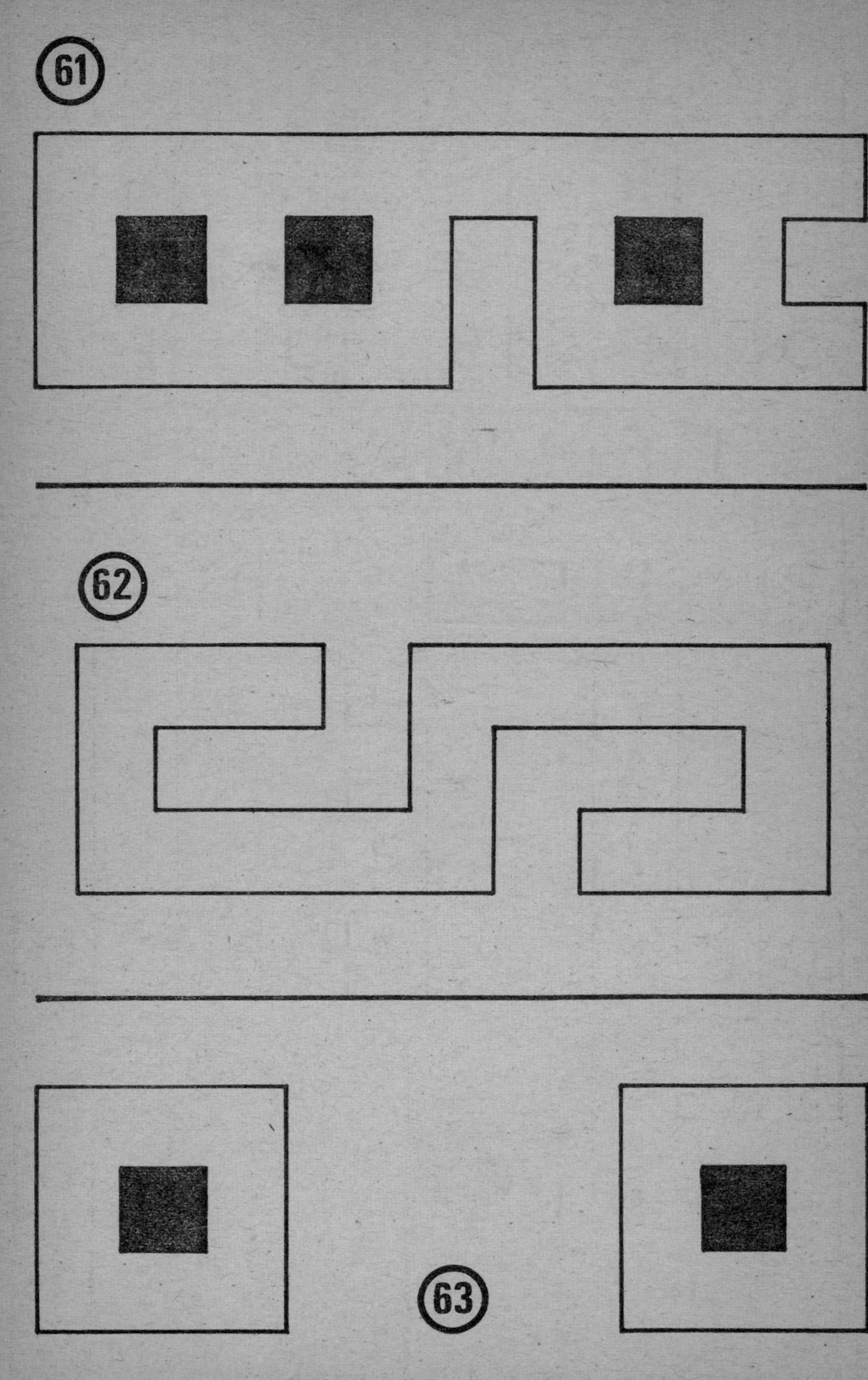

63

DODO BREAD

WED END SOB ROD RYE

STRAWBERRY

PIPER DIG

DAY DIP FAR

DRY FOUND

GAG DOG

BOW WAG RAG BAD BOG

BAR

64

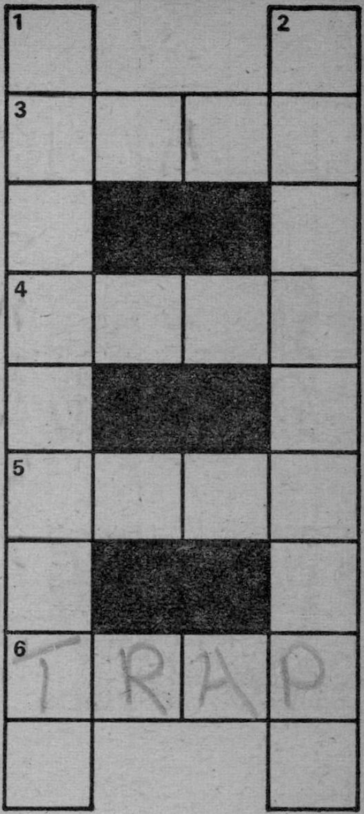

ACROSS

3. Find the fine, brave man hidden in the letters of this sentence: ANN LIKES HER OLD DOLLS BEST.
4. To shout to somebody, or to ring up somebody on the telephone.
5. You walk in this awkward way if you have hurt one of your feet.
6. If there were mice in your house you would put this down to try and catch them.

DOWN

1. It is sweet and brown and comes in bars.
2. They are sweet and round and come on sticks.

65

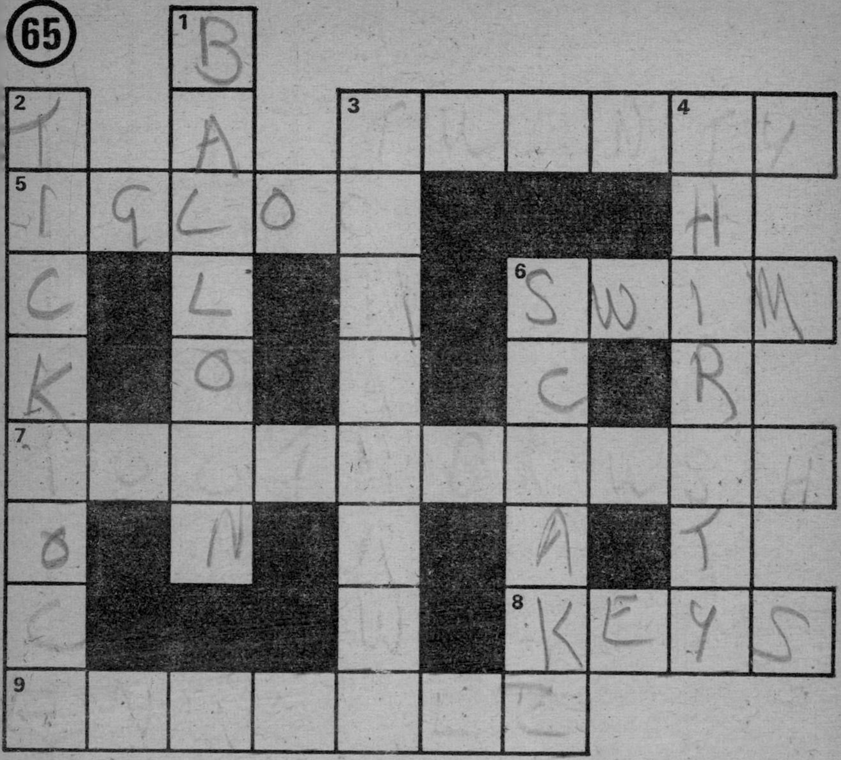

ACROSS

3. Four fives make this number.
5. An Eskimo snow house.
6. What you do to move your body through water.
7. You clean your teeth with this.
8. They unlock locks.
9. The bump where your finger bends.

DOWN

1. We blow it up, usually for a party.
2. The noise a clock makes.
3. A Red Indian weapon like an axe.
4. How you feel when you want something to drink.
6. Dogs and cats love you to do this to their backs.

Making Music

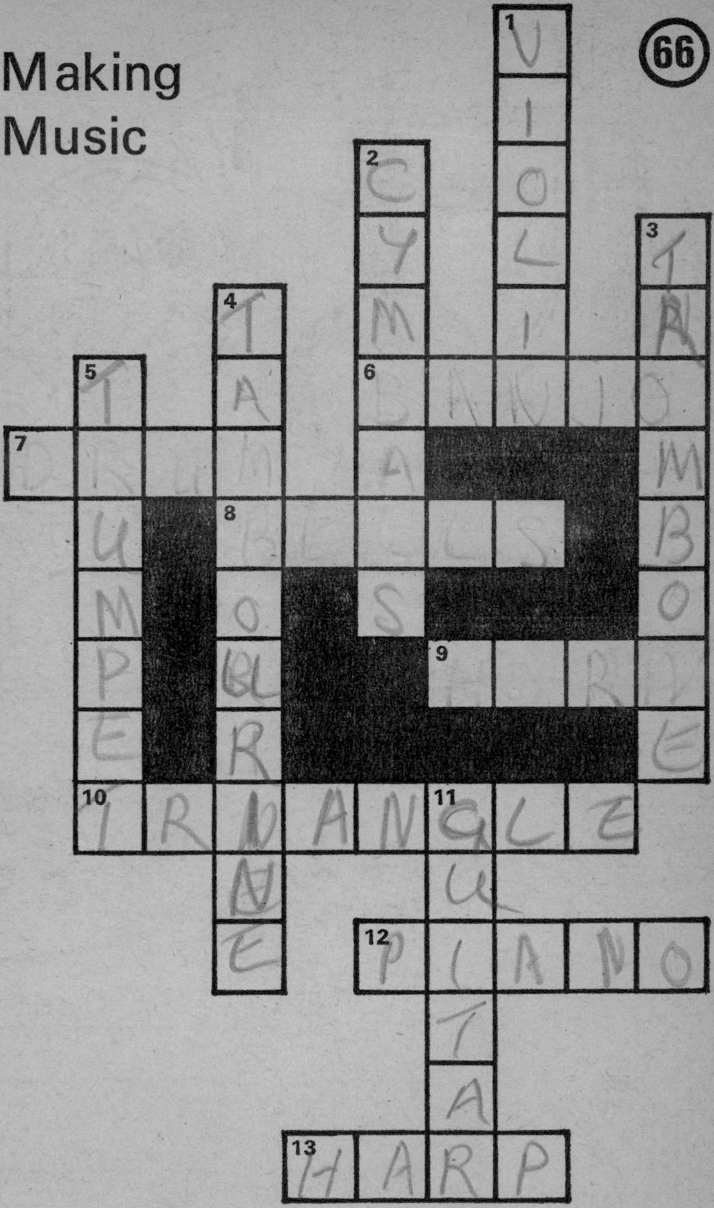

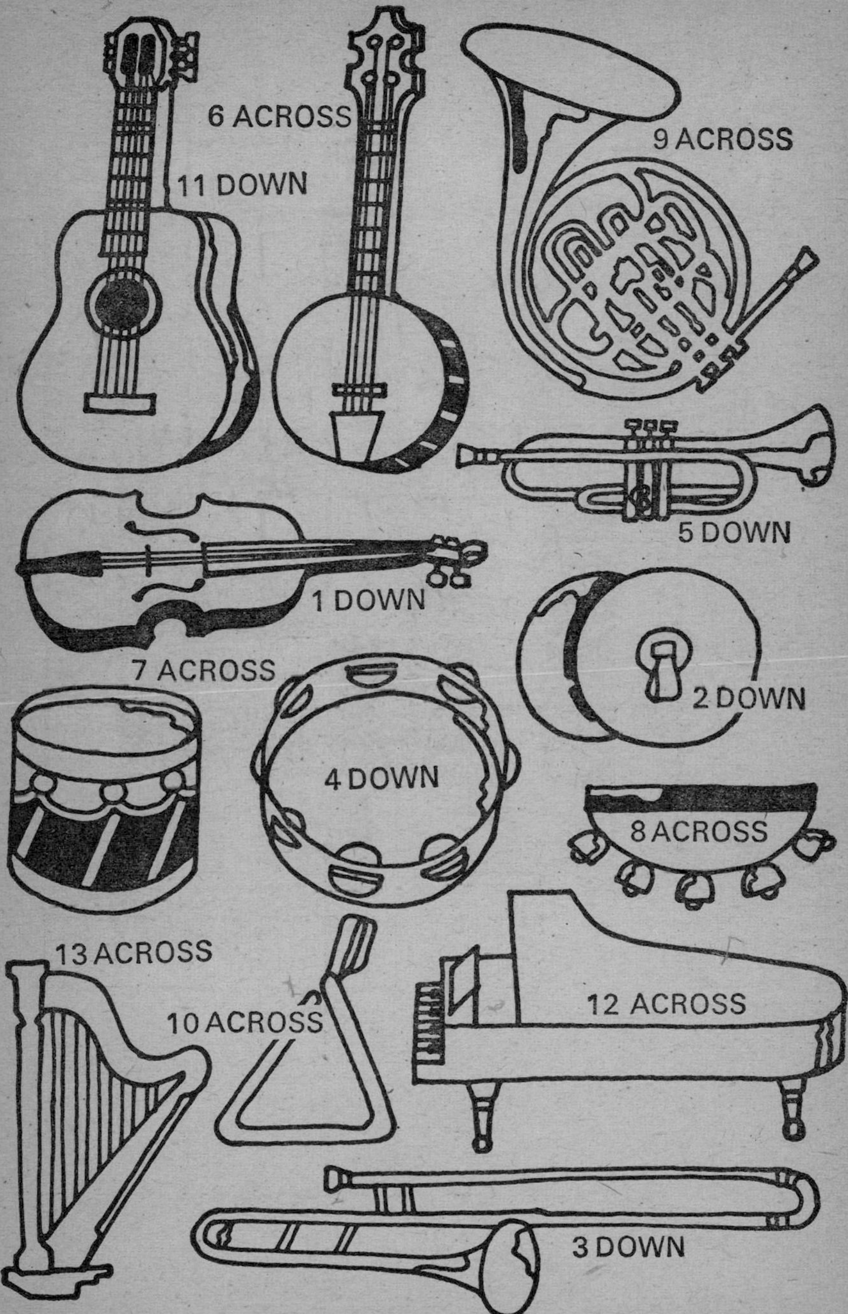
6 ACROSS
9 ACROSS
11 DOWN
5 DOWN
1 DOWN
7 ACROSS
2 DOWN
4 DOWN
8 ACROSS
13 ACROSS
12 ACROSS
10 ACROSS
3 DOWN

67

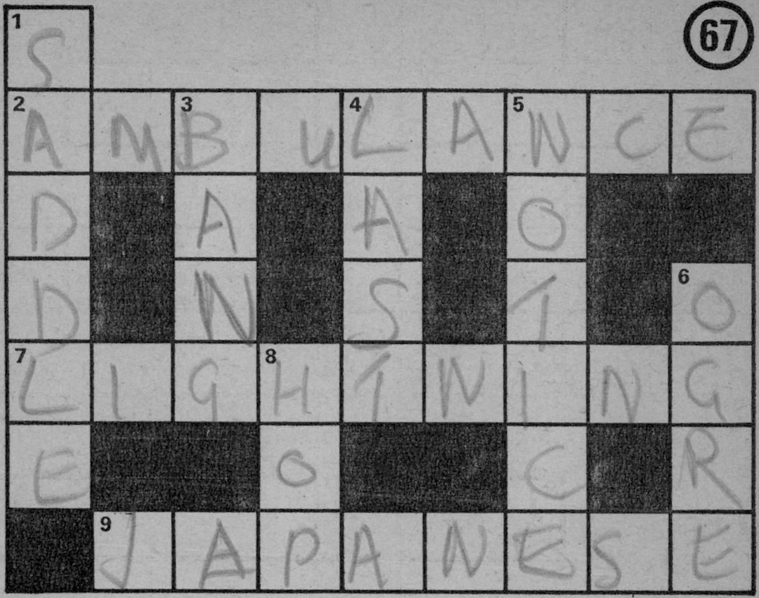

ACROSS

2. A special car that takes people to hospital.
7. You see this just before you hear thunder.
9. A person who comes from Japan.

DOWN

1. This sits on a horse and the rider sits on it.
3. A loud noise.
4. The opposite of FIRST.
5. A word for a sign like 'Keep Off The Grass'. Its anagram is NICE TO.
6. A horrible giant. His anagram is GORE.
8. What you do when you jump along on one foot.

68

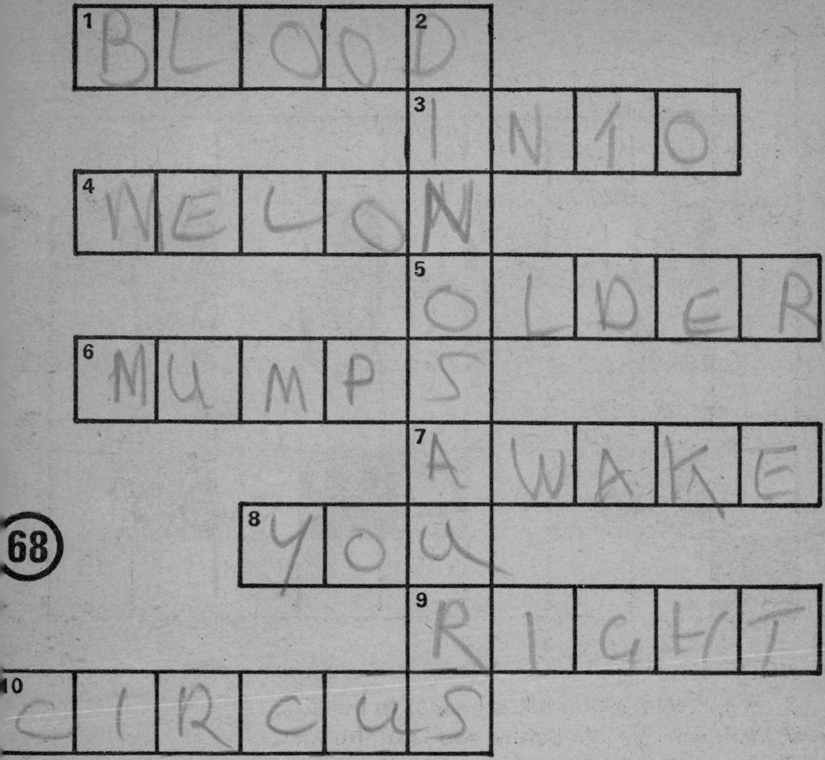

ACROSS

1. It comes out if you cut yourself.
3. The opposite of OUT OF.
4. A big fruit. Its anagram is LEMON.
5. The opposite of YOUNGER.
6. An illness that gives you swellings at the sides of your face.
7. The opposite of ASLEEP.
8. Spell this answer by taking the first letter of each of these words: YELLOW ONIONS UNDERGROUND.
9. The opposite of WRONG.
10. A show where you see clowns, acrobats and elephants.

DOWN

2. These enormous animals lived on earth millions of years ago.

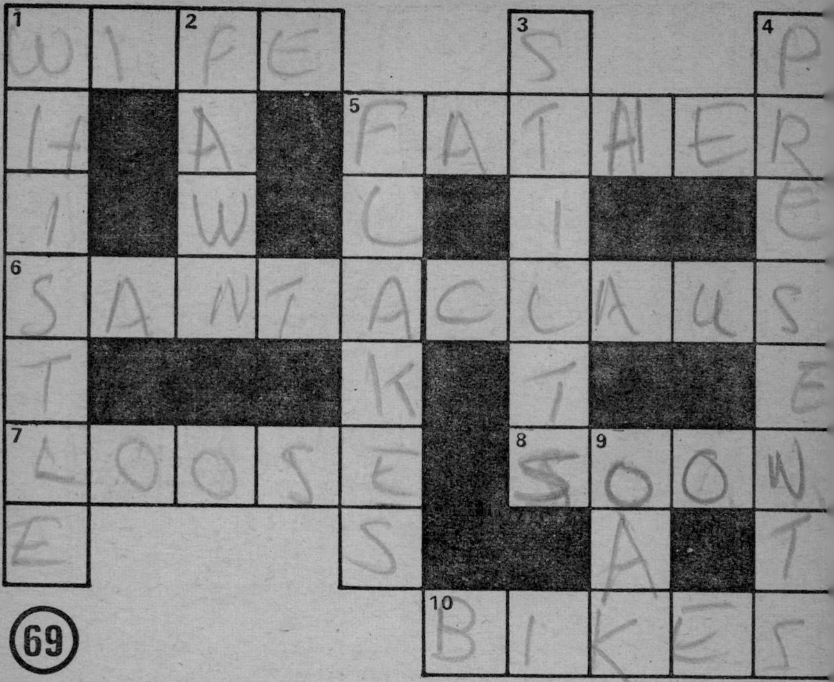

69

ACROSS

1. A married man is called a HUSBAND. What is a married woman called?
5. And this man is married to MOTHER.
6. He fills stockings at Christmas.
7. The opposite of TIGHT.
8. In a short time.
10. A short word for BICYCLES.

DOWN

1. A sharp noise made by blowing through your lips or teeth.
2. A baby deer.
3. Tall sticks to balance on and walk on.
4. The answer to 6 Across brings these.
5. Little bits of falling snow.
9. Acorns grow on this tree.

70

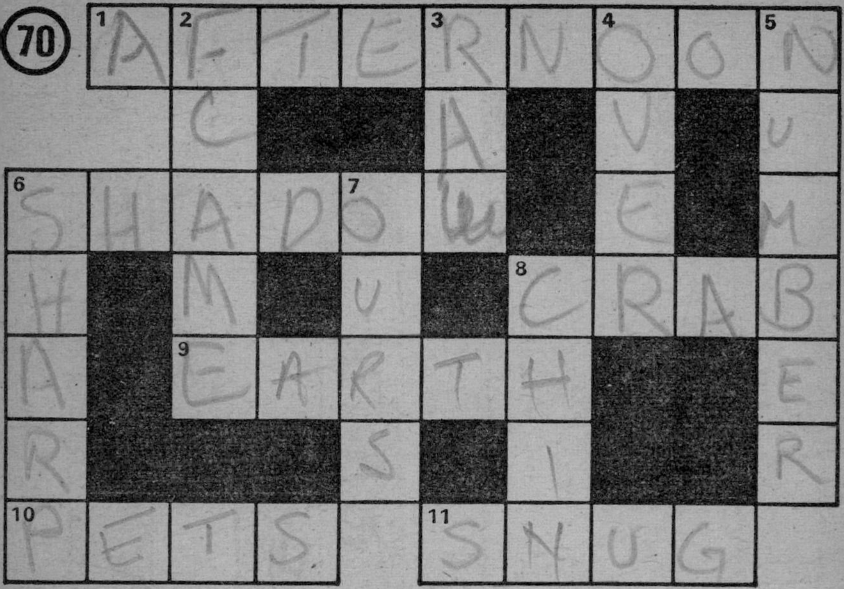

ACROSS

1. The part of the day between morning and evening.
6. Stand with your back to the sun and you will see this dark shape of yourself on the ground.
8. A sea animal with claws.
9. Plants must keep their roots in this. Its anagram is HEART.
10. Lions and tigers are WILD animals. What kind of animals are cows and dogs?
11. GUNS backwards makes this word, which means 'warm and comfortable'.

DOWN

2. The hot bright thing on top of a burning candle.
3. The opposite of COOKED.
4. The opposite of UNDER.
5. What we call 3 or 10 or 20.
6. Sugar tastes like this.
7. If YOUR pen is YOURS, what is OUR pen?
8. This is at the bottom of your face.

(71)

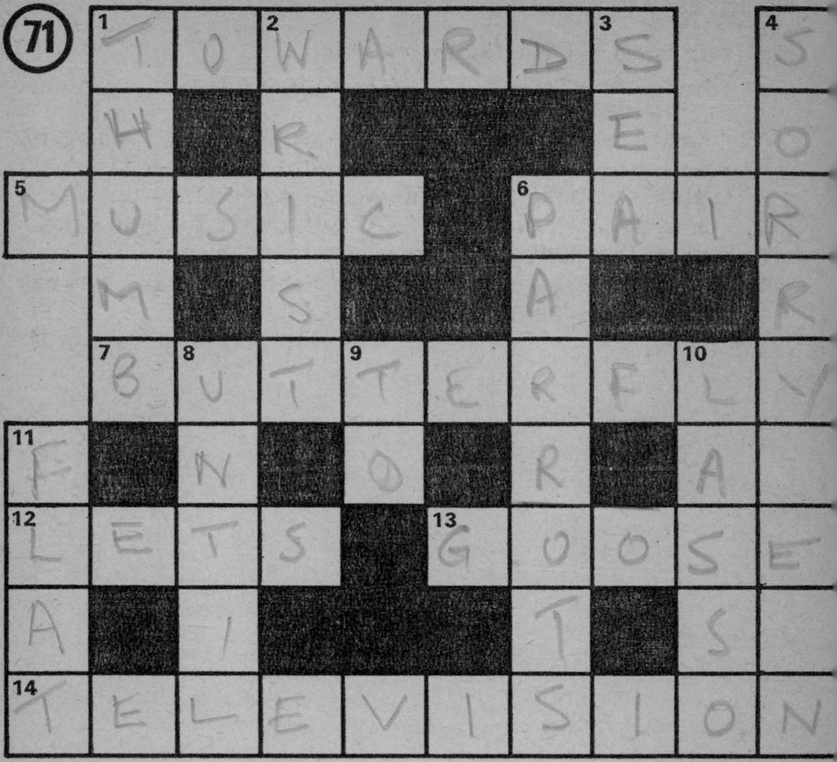

ACROSS

1. You can walk AWAY FROM something or you can walk – – – – – – – – it. An anagram for this word is WAS TROD.
5. The sound played by a band or an orchestra.
6. The special word for TWO that we use when we are talking about shoes or socks or gloves.
7. An insect with big beautiful wings.
12. The short way of saying LET US.
13. A big farm bird with a long neck. It eats grass and it hisses.
14. You watch this in colour or in black and white.

DOWN

1. Your hand has four fingers and this.
2. This comes between your hand and your arm.
3. Another word for 'ocean'.
4. What we say when we have hurt someone without meaning to.
6. These birds have bright colours and they often talk.
8. UNLIT is an anagram for this word, which means 'up to'.
9. Take the STAIN out of the STATION to find this little word.
10. A circle of rope that a cowboy uses to catch cattle.
11. This word means 'smooth', and 'without any bumps'. You can find it among the letters of UNINFLATIONARY.

72

ACROSS

1. If you split something into four pieces and each piece is the same size, what is each piece called?
6. People bake pies and roast meat in this part of the cooker.
7. The opposite of LATE.
8. Long thin stuff that we use to tie up parcels.
9. The thing like a finger that is on your foot.
10. It is bigger than a village but smaller than a city.
12. The opposite of IN.

14. A very strong wind. Its anagram is A LEG.
17. These things are made from two slices of bread with something like meat in between.

DOWN

1. These ask us for answers.
2. EAGER is an anagram of this word, which means to think the same way someone else thinks.
3. A place where you can buy things specially made for children to play with.
4. If you hear a lion doing this you know he is angry.
5. You guide a horse with these.
11. Fishermen catch fish in them.
13. Write NOT backwards for a heavy weight.
15. This is left after a fire has burned paper or wood.
16. 'DO, RE, – –, FA, SOL, LA, TI, DO.'

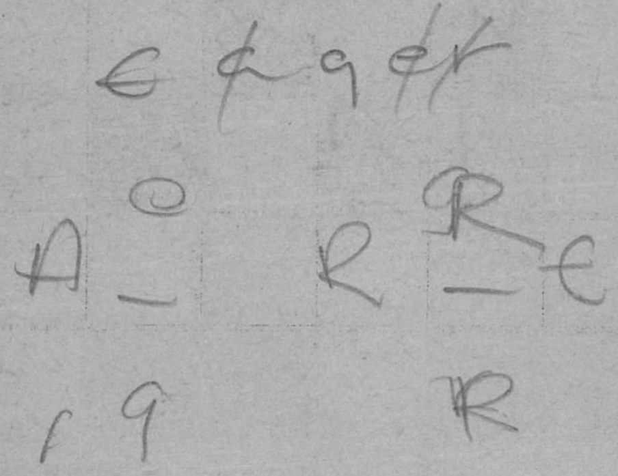

73

ACROSS

1. Another word for LITTLE.
4. To turn round and round very quickly.
8. The opposite of DOWNSTAIRS.
9. This animal has antlers on its head.
11. A merry-go-round at a fair is also called a ROUND – – – – –.
12. We use this little word when we are not sure. You can find it in RIFLE and in STIFF.
13. PAR backwards spells a kind of knock.
14. Twenty added to thirty.
15. An old word for a story. Its anagram is LATE.
17. The opposite of SELL.
18. What an actor does.
20. An arch of many colours in the sky.
23. What we breathe.
24. We make castles with this at the beach.
25. WAL – – –, BRAZIL – – –, PEA – – – The same word is missing each time. What is it?

DOWN

2. It shows towns and roads and helps us get from one place to another.
3. The opposite of EARLIER.
5. A place where we can buy stamps and send parcels.
6. Something that happens every day happens DAILY. Something that happens every night happens – – – – – – – –.
7. A big animal with a very long neck.
8. The opposite of OVER.
10. The opposite of FULL.
16. A sheep's baby.
17. A fire does this.
19. A weapon like a big knife.
21. If you do this with your head you mean 'Yes.'
22. To have something which is only yours.
23. 'We didn't go out. We stayed – – home.'

74

ACROSS

1. A hot, wild place where monkeys and elephants live.
6. It has sixty minutes in it.
7. The kind of doors you find in fences.
8. You must buy this if you want to travel on a train or a bus.
11. The opposite of DEAD.
12. They take care of people in hospitals.
13. The noise an unhappy person makes by letting his breath out.
15. A thing that is no use at all is this.
17. Write TOPS backwards for a dirty mark.
19. A set of people taught by one teacher.
22. If you have a lot of money you are this.
23. '– – – – – in Wonderland.'
24. Glue, gum, toffee and honey are this.

DOWN

1. These puzzles are made of little pieces which you fit together into a picture.
2. When you have this to do, you don't do anything.
3. You must do this hard if you want to hear a very soft sound.
4. If you do this to a door nobody else can open it.
5. A horse goes at this speed when it is moving faster than a walk.
9. These shapes are round.
10. 'What do you choose? ODDS or – – – – –?'
14. A house made for a rabbit.
16. Something you have promised not to tell.
18. INAPT is an anagram for something we use to make pictures.
20. The opposite of AT HOME.
21. What you do when you keep swinging a rope over your head and jumping over it.

Answers to Numbered Puzzles

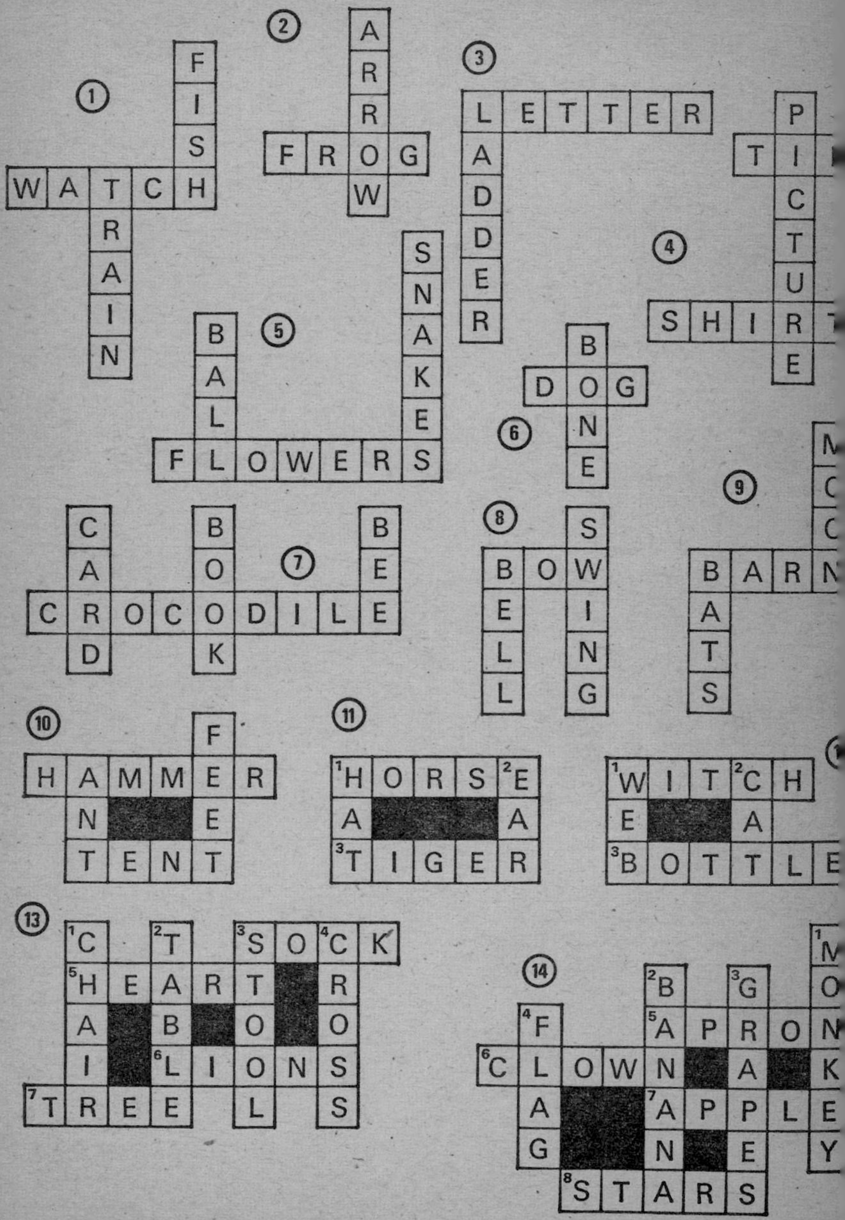

15

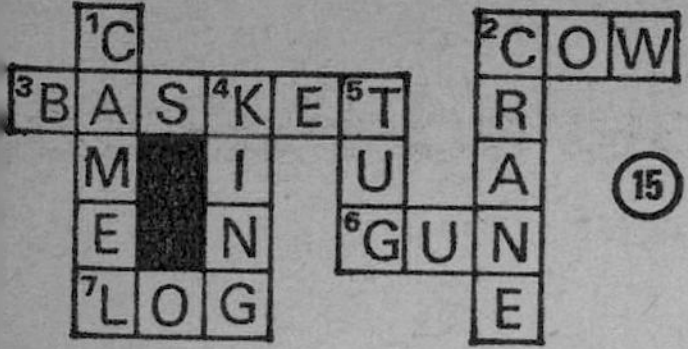

16

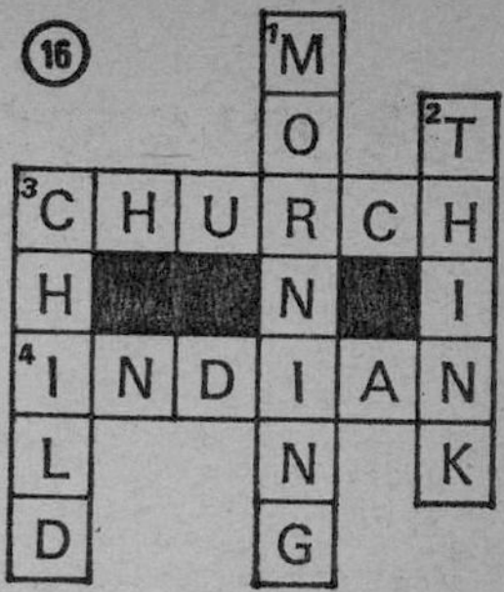

17

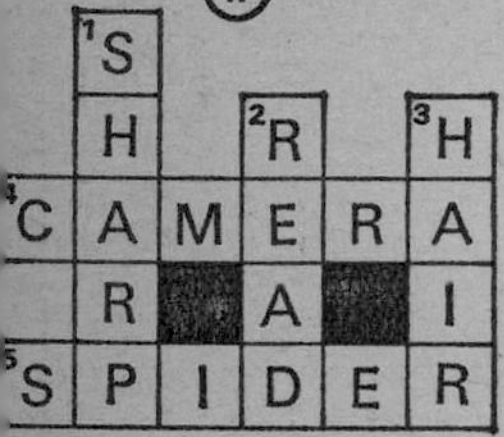

18

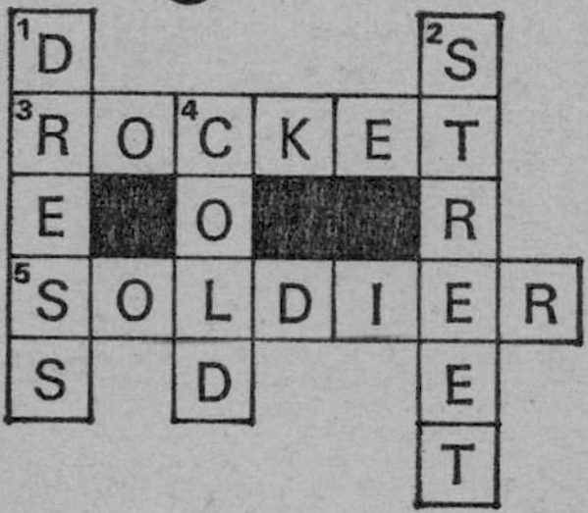

19

20

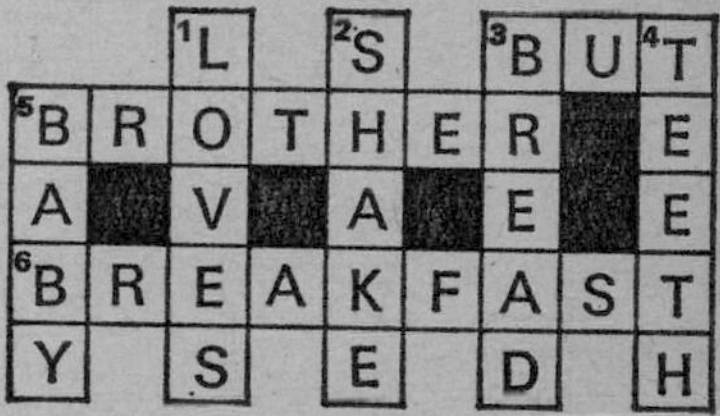

21

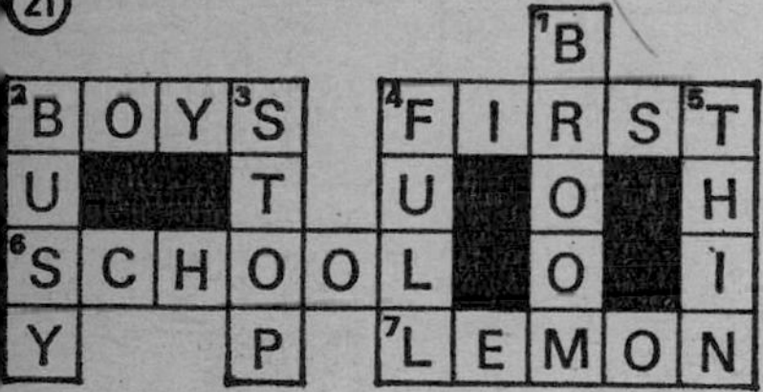

22

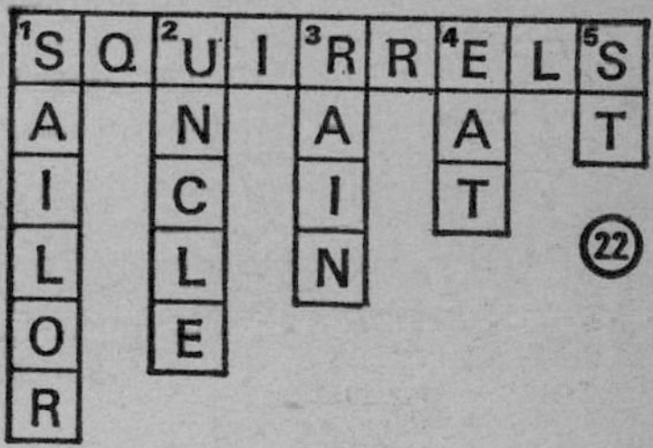

23

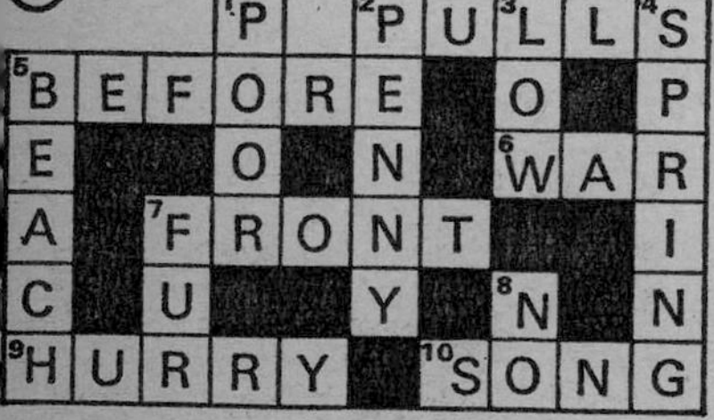

24

25

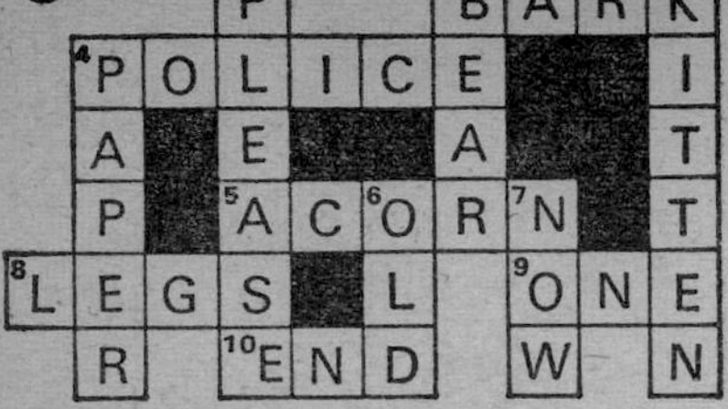

26

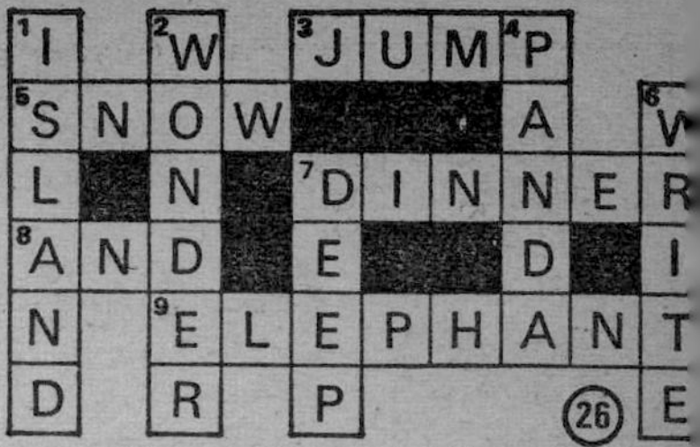

27

28

29

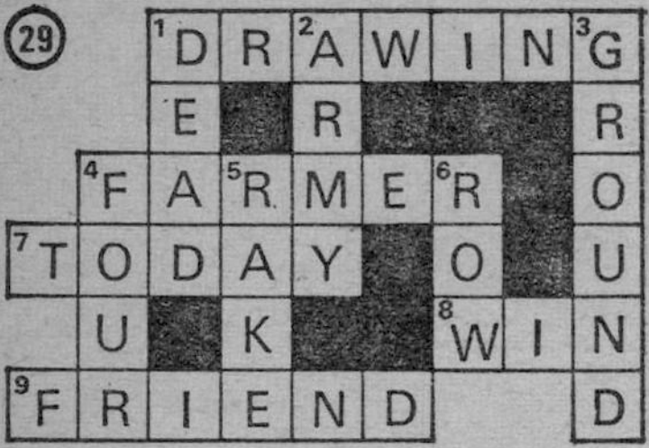

30

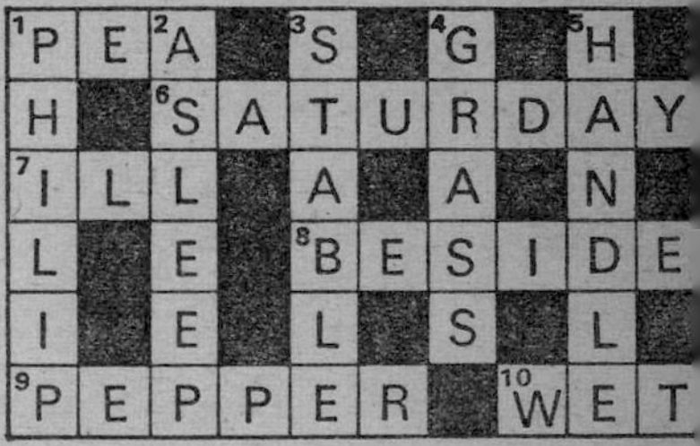

31

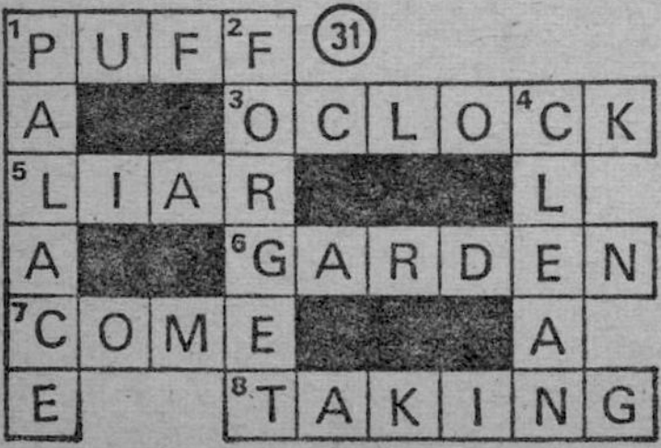

32

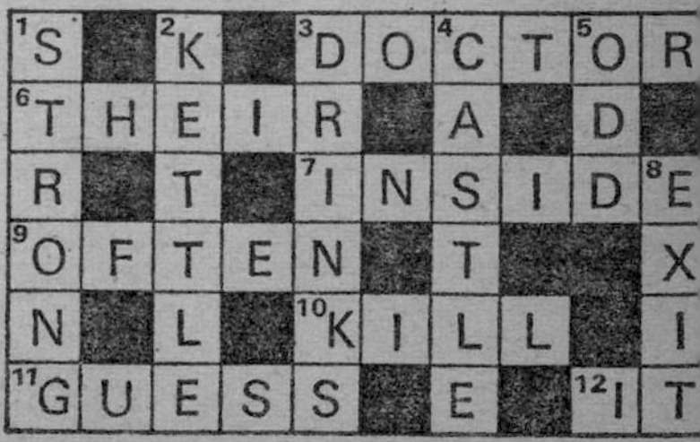

33
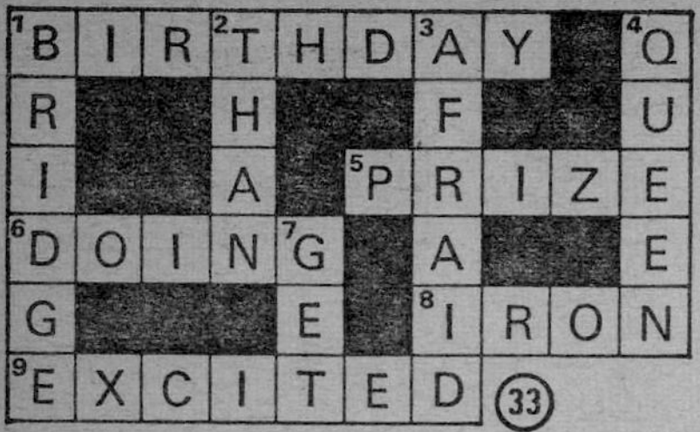

34
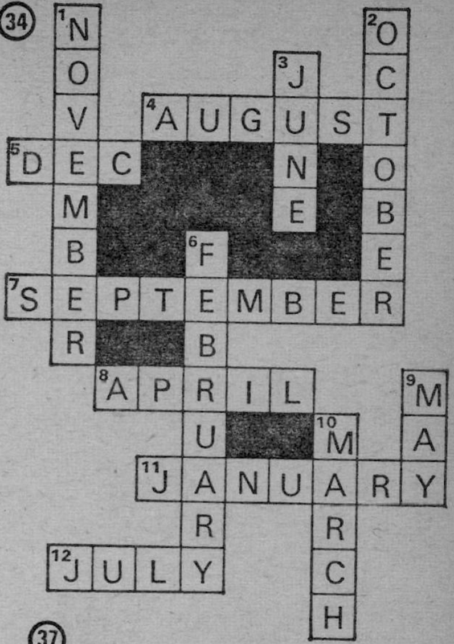

35
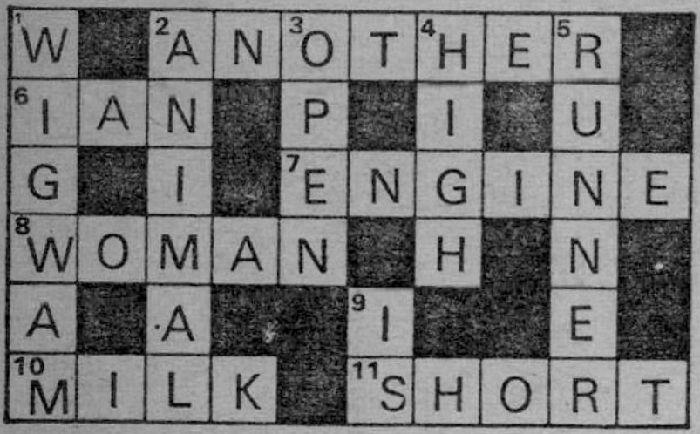

36
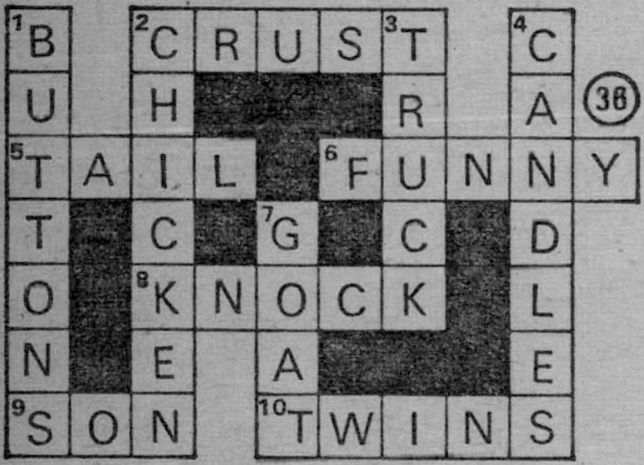

37
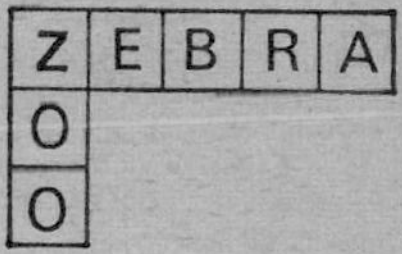

38
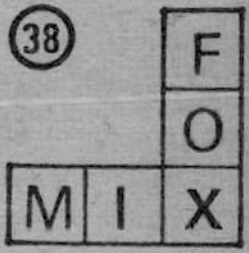

39
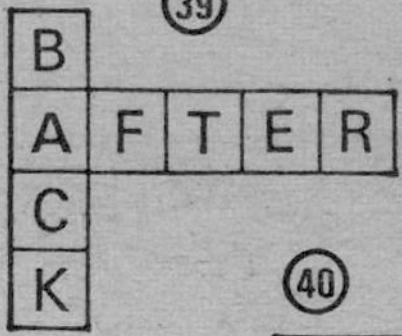

40
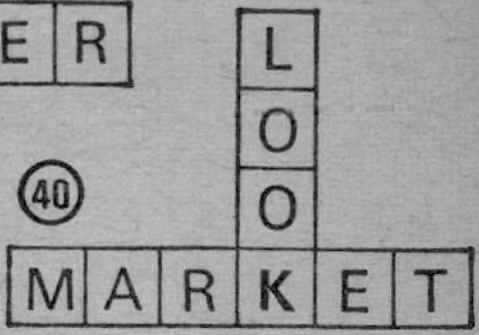

41

42
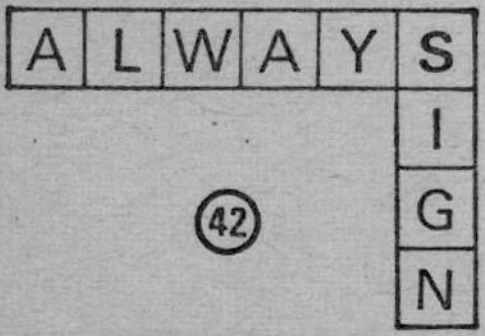

43

44
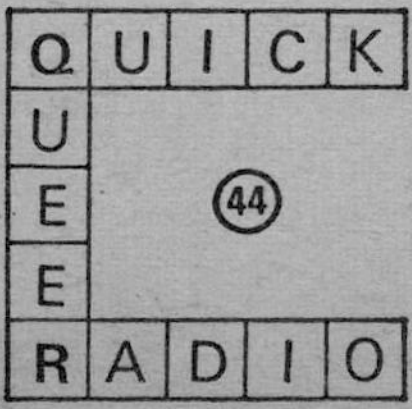

45
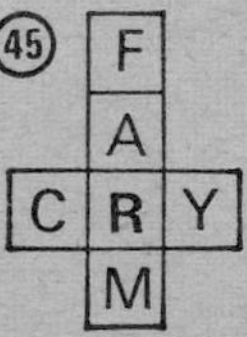

46
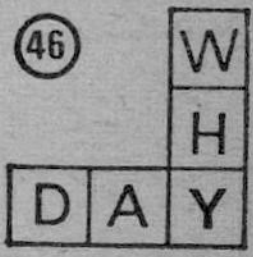

47

48

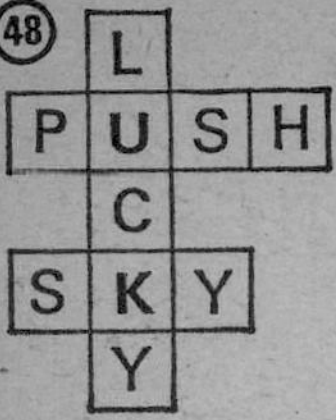

49

50

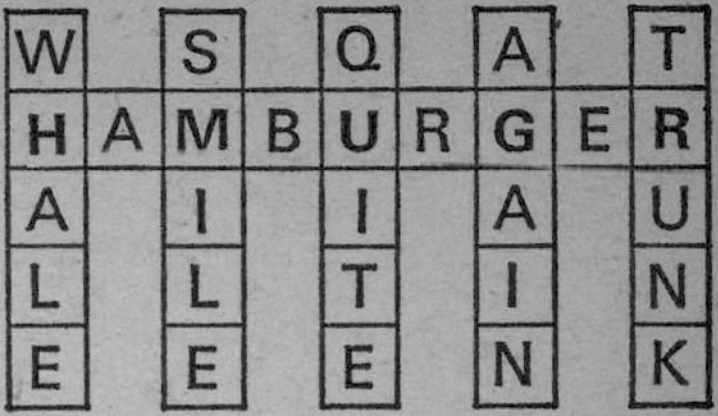

51

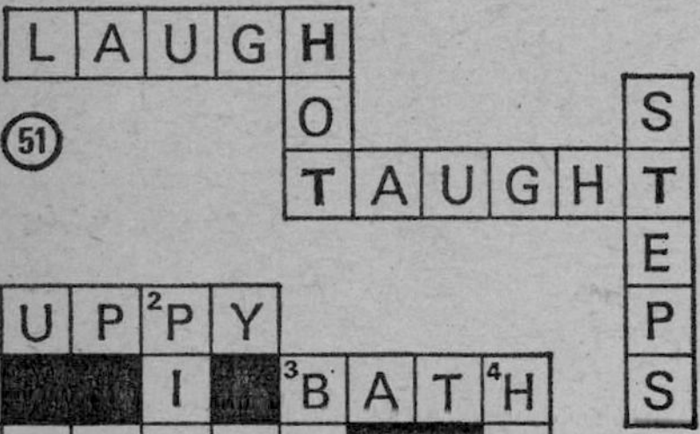

52

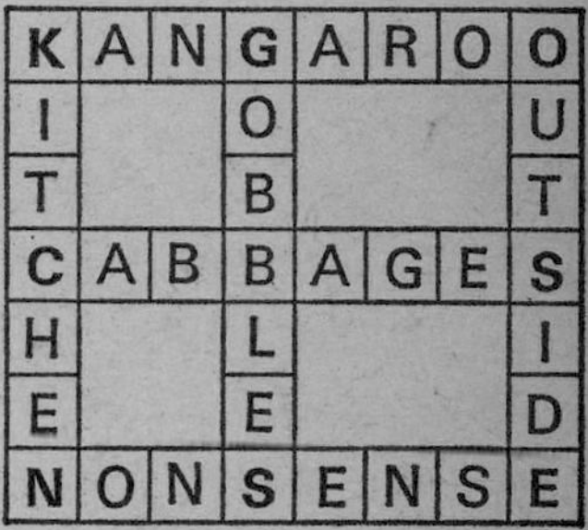

53

54

55

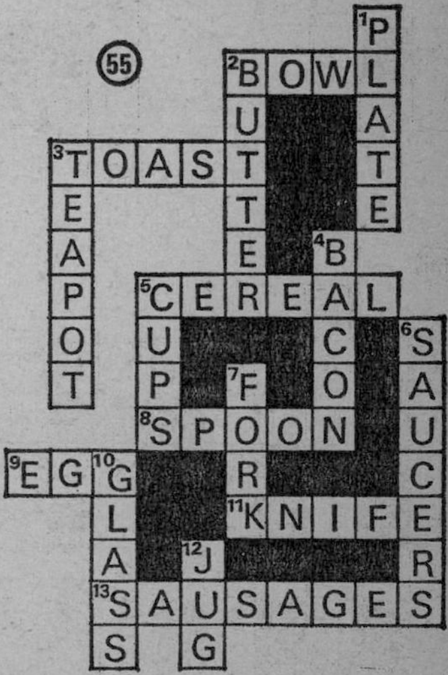

56

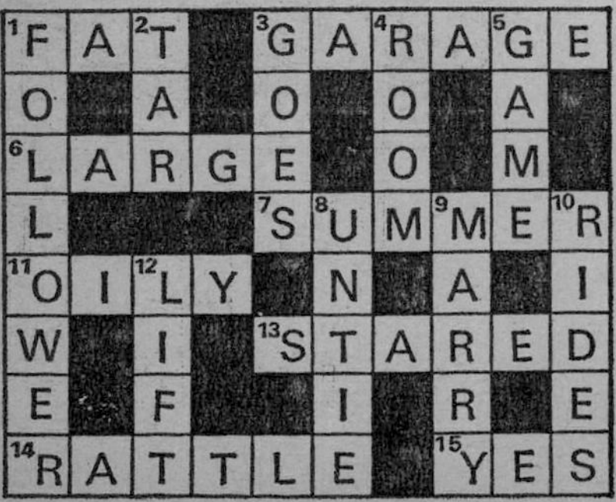

57

	T	
W	A	X
	N	

58

	D	O	T
		U	
S	E	T	

59

T	I	P
I	■	A
N	U	T

60

			R	E	C	O	R	D
			I	■	A			
K	N	I	G	H	T			

61

S	T	R	A	W	B	E	R	R	Y
O	■	Y	■	E		N	■	O	
B	R	E	A	D		D	O	D	O

62

D	I	G		F	O	U	N	D
I				A				A
P	I	P	E	R		D	R	Y

B	O	W
O	■	A
G	A	G

63

B	A	R
A	■	A
D	O	G

64

1C			2L
3H	E	R	O
O	■	■	L
4C	A	L	L
O	■	■	I
5L	I	M	P
A	■	■	O
6T	R	A	P
E			S

65

		1B							
2T		A		3T	W	E	N	4T	Y
5I	G	L	O	O	■	■	■	H	
C	■	L	■	M	■	6S	W	I	M
K	■	O	■	A	■	T	■	R	
7T	O	O	T	H	B	R	U	S	H
O	■	N	■	A	■	O	■	T	
C	■	■	■	W	■	8K	E	Y	S
9K	N	U	C	K	L	E			

66

							1V		
							I		
					2C		O		
					Y		L		3T
			4T		M		I		R
	5T		A		6B	A	N	J	O
7D	R	U	M		A	■	■	■	M
	U	■	8B	E	L	L	S	■	B
	M	■	O	■	S	■	■	■	O
	P	■	U	■	■	9H	O	R	N
	E	■	R	■	■	■	■	■	E
	10T	R	I	A	N	11G	L	E	
			N			U			
			E		12P	I	A	N	O
						T			
						A			
				13H	A	R	P		

67
S
AMBULANCE
D A A O
D N S T O
LIGHTNING
E O C R
JAPANESE

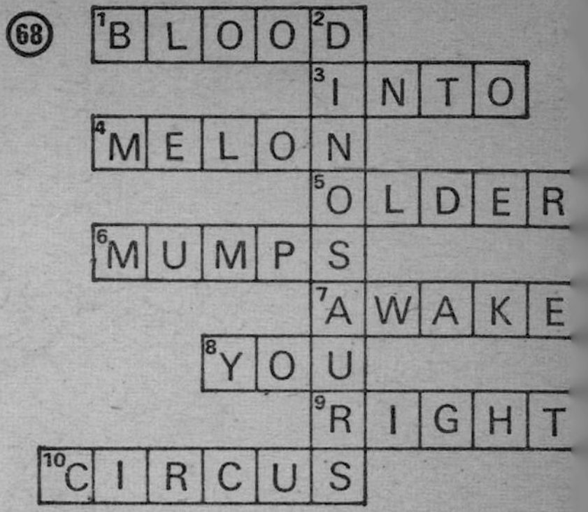
68
BLOOD
INTO
MELON
OLDER
MUMPS
AWAKE
YOU
RIGHT
CIRCUS

69
WIFE S P
H A FATHER
I W L I E
SANTACLAUS
T K T E
LOOSE SOON
E S A T
BIKES

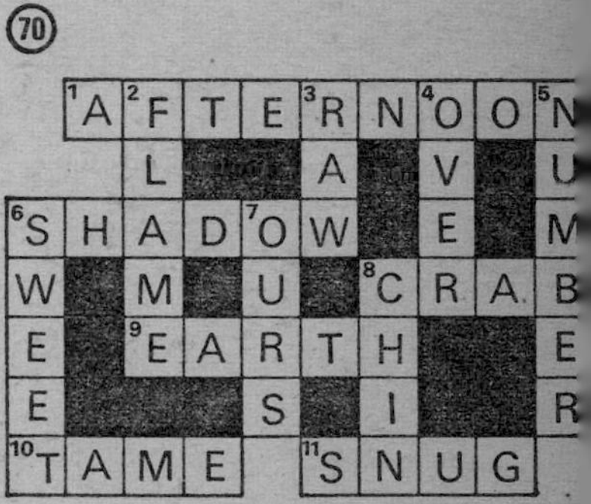
70
AFTERNOON
L A V U
SHADOW E M
W M U CRAB
E EARTH E
E S I R
TAME SNUG

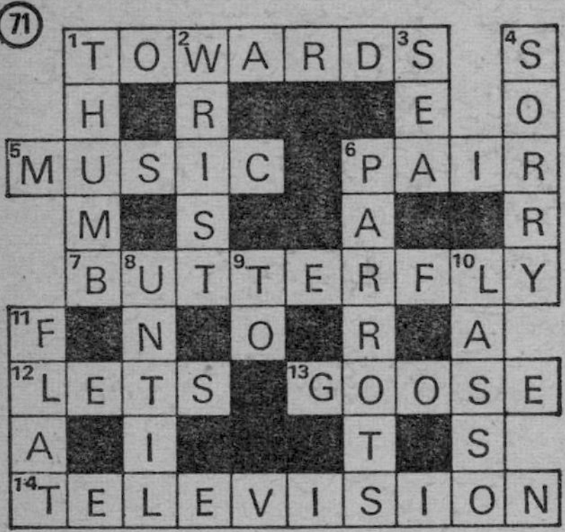
71
TOWARDS S
H R E O
MUSIC PAIR
M S A R
BUTTERFLY
F N O R A
LETS GOOSE
A I T S
TELEVISION

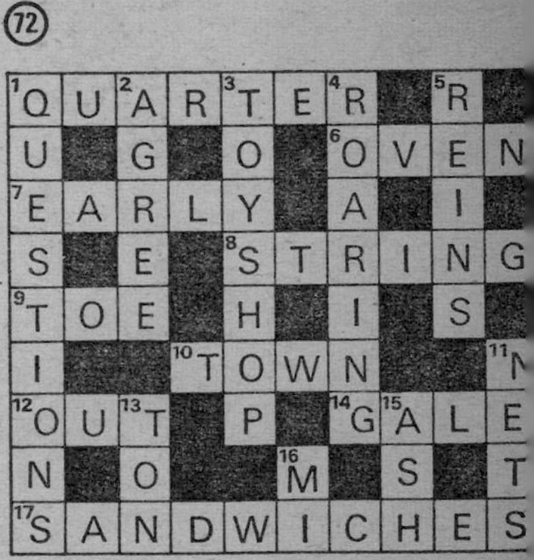
72
QUARTER R
U G O OVEN
EARLY A I
S E STRING
TOE H I S
I TOWN
OUT P GALE
N O M S T
SANDWICHES

73

1 S	2 M	A	3 L	L	■	4 S	5 P	I	6 N
■	A	■	A	■	7 G	■	O	■	I
8 U	P	S	T	A	I	R	S	■	G
N	■	■	E	■	R	■	T	■	H
9 D	E	10 E	R	■	11 A	B	O	U	T
E	■	M	■	12 I	F	■	F	■	L
13 R	A	P	■	■	14 F	I	F	T	Y
■	■	15 T	A	16 L	E	■	I	■	■
17 B	U	Y	■	A	■	18 A	C	T	19 S
U	■	■	■	M	■	■	E	■	W
20 R	A	I	21 N	B	22 O	W	■	■	O
N	■	■	O	■	W	■	23 A	I	R
24 S	A	N	D	■	25 N	U	T	■	D

74

1 J	U	2 N	G	3 L	E	■	4 L	■	5 T
I	■	O	■	I	■	6 H	O	U	R
7 G	A	T	E	S	■	■	C	■	O
S	■	H	■	8 T	I	9 C	K	10 E	T
11 A	L	I	V	E	■	I	■	V	■
W	■	N	■	12 N	U	R	S	E	S
13 S	I	G	14 H	■	■	C	■	N	■
■	■	■	15 U	S	E	L	E	S	16 S
17 S	18 P	O	T	■	■	E	■	■	E
■	A	■	19 C	L	20 A	S	21 S	■	C
22 R	I	C	H	■	W	■	K	■	R
■	N	■	■	■	23 A	L	I	C	E
24 S	T	I	C	K	Y	■	P	■	T

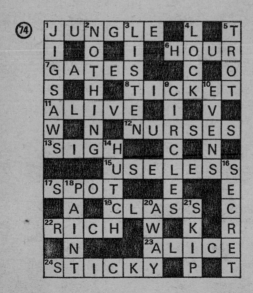